RAISE YOUR PRICES, ATTRACT MORE BUSINESS

ALSO BY RICK OTT:

Creating Demand

Creating Demand
(audio program)

Practical Wisdom

Unleashing Your Productivity
(audio program)

RAISE YOUR PRICES, ATTRACT MORE BUSINESS

The Pricing Power Playbook

RICK OTT

Ocean View Communications
A division of Symmetric Systems, Inc.
OceanViewCommunications.com

Written by: Rick Ott
Edited by: Jeanne Ott
Cover design: Ott & Associates

Ocean View is a registered trademark of Symmetric Systems, Inc.

Printed in the United States of America

ISBN: 978-0-9663491-6-0

Contents:

Preface

As a consumer, I love discount retailers. Walmart, The Home Depot, Costco, Kohl's, OfficeMax, Amazon.com and a bunch of others. Good quality and good prices. Aren't they wonderful?

I love low-price services, too. Southwest Airlines, McDonald's, The Vanguard Group, Expedia.com, all those cheap apps from Apple's App Store, the 99-cent dry cleaner that opened near me recently, and others. Good quality and good prices. What would we do without them?

From the business person's perspective, it's obvious that the low price philosophy is a viable, proven way to go, as the above mentioned companies attribute. When your company is founded upon the principle of delivering the lowest possible price to the buyer*, and you become adept at managing your expenses, you can do very well with this approach.

However, I don't believe that the low price approach is best for every business. There are a good number of businesses, from large to small, that enjoy success by avoiding the low price game entire-

---

*The terms "buyer," "customer," "consumer," and "client" are used synonymously and interchangeably in this book.

ly and charging higher prices. In some cases, considerably higher prices.

If your chosen route to business success is through low prices, then I'm sure there are plenty of other more useful books than this one that will help you win at that game. But if you favor the higher price route to success, you're reading the right book.

What This Book Is Not About

With a title like *Raise Your Prices, Attract More Business*, it's incumbent upon me to clarify exactly what this book is about and what it's not about before we go any further, lest some reader somewhere be smitten with misconception.

This book is *not* about:

- Instigating inflation.
- Cheating, conning, or ripping off.
- Price gouging.
- Greed.

In fact, if you have a tendency to engage in any of these activities, you're going to get yourself into deep trouble sooner or later. And when that happens, don't blame me. The strategies presented here are for purposes other than the miscreant.

Nor is it my intent to mount some sort of price-raising crusade or business liberation movement. I just thought you would appreciate, and make judicial use of, additional revenue, additional net income, and additional happy customers. Simple as that.

Finally, it's not my intent to present you with an array of new, never-before-heard-of concepts. (Although, lo and behold, some new stuff has crept in.) I'd much rather round up, codify, analyze, and simplify preexisting information in a way that makes it both usable and effective for you.

What This Book is Really About

This book is really about (a) presenting you with proven, practical strategies that work, and (b) stimulating your creativity to adopt strategies you are not currently using and adapt them to your particular situation.

It's also about selection. I've taken a smorgasbord approach, laying out thirteen different strategies that may or may not be right for you. Out of thirteen, choose the one, two, or three that are right for you at any given time.

The Underlying Tenets

The entire concept of raising your prices and simultaneously attracting more business is based upon two primary tenets:

Primary Tenet Number One:
If it doesn't benefit the buyer, it won't work.

Why should the buyer spend more money with you if doing so isn't in his or her best interest? They shouldn't. Therefore, it's incumbent upon you to make it beneficial to the buyer to spend more money with you, which is exactly what you'll be doing when you implement the strategies presented here.

Primary Tenet Number Two:
People will pay more provided they get more.

If this weren't true, Cadillac, Lincoln, Lexus, Mercedes, and Land Rover wouldn't sell any vehicles. FedEx and UPS wouldn't deliver any packages, Nike wouldn't sell any shoes, and Disneyland and Disneyworld wouldn't have any visitors. If this weren't true, Philips wouldn't sell any Sonicare toothbrushes, Starbucks wouldn't sell a cup of coffee, and Carl's Jr. and Hardee's wouldn't sell any Monster Thickburgers.

But it is true. People do buy millions of dollars worth of these products each and every year, despite the availability of lower-priced alternatives. People are happy to pay more provided they get more.

Certainly there are buyers who seek the lowest possible price no matter what. These people are not your target market. There are, however, a huge number of people that want more and are willing to pay for it. These people are your target market.

The question is, of course, what constitutes the "more" that people are willing to pay for? Or from your standpoint, what is the "more" that you deliver, which allows you to charge a higher price?

The "more" you deliver can fall into one or more of these categories:

1. Greater quantity of product.
2. Higher quality product.
3. Better, faster service.
4. Greater psychological satisfaction.

We will discuss all four, but the one I will give the most attention to is number 4. Since psychological satisfaction is the least understood of the bunch, the toughest to get a handle on, the most difficult to implement, and yet is highly transferable into higher prices when used correctly, that is the "more" we'll favor.

Everyone Wins With Higher Prices

Higher prices can benefit everyone involved — the company and its management, the employees, the owners, and suppliers. Higher prices can benefit the customer too. How so? Let me illustrate with the True Tale of Two Radio Stations.

In the mid-1970s, as a young guy fresh out of college, I was hired by a rock 'n roll radio station in Norfolk, Virginia to do the 7pm-to-midnight air shift. I had worked my way through Michigan State as both a graphic artist and disc jockey, and decided to pursue the more fun of the two, radio. An undiscriminating send-out of audition tapes landed me the Norfolk gig. So in September of 1974 I loaded practically everything I owned into my 1968 Chevrolet station wagon and drove from Detroit (my home town) to Norfolk.

I'll never forget the shock and dismay I felt upon seeing my new place of employment for the first time. Actually, everyday I showed up for work I shook my head in disbelief.

This Norfolk radio station, which was actually located across the Elizabeth River in Portsmouth, Virginia, was the most dilapidated, gutted facility I'd ever seen, or even dreamed could exist. It was a small white shack with most of the ceiling tiles missing, and buckets all over the floor to catch leaking rain water, or worse. One day a snake fell out of the ceiling and right into one of these buckets on the receptionist's desk. She ran screaming out the front door and never returned. (Why we even had a receptionist to begin with was a mystery to me. No one from the outside world ever came to this place, and the phone hardly ever rang.) Once word of this "snake attack" spread, other members of the staff began showing up with weapons of defense, such as baseball bats and tire irons. One female disc jockey began bringing a loaded pistol to work, which seemed somewhat extreme at the time, but may not have been such a bad idea in retrospect, considering this dump was in a dark, desolate part of town and she worked by herself late at night. Luckily she never mistook me for a snake or other predator.

The furnishing — what little of it they had — were World War II vintage, as was most of the equipment. The on-air studio had no chair or stool. The news director let us keep some cartons of teletype paper there, and that's what we sat on. At some point the studio clock must have fallen off the wall, because by the time I arrived it was lying horizontally on the floor underneath the main console, and no one, including myself, ever bothered to re-hang it.

When cold weather set in, we discovered the furnace wasn't working, and the owner was in no hurry to have it fixed. We just worked in coats and gloves.

To be accurate, I should mention that the ownership of this dilapidated station was in the process of building new offices and studios in downtown Norfolk, which we did indeed move into a few months later. It was a big improvement in the physical facility, without question. Yet the physical facility was only one aspect of this poor radio station's condition.

The owner was financially weak and managerially poor. The company was anything but stable. Salaries were pitiful.

The station had no ratings. None. Didn't even show up in the ratings. Which meant practically no one was listening. I was one of a bunch of new guys they brought in to turn this turkey around, and we did have some success in that regard. By that spring we'd increased listenership over 130 percent, which meant we were now showing up in the ratings, albeit still near the bottom. We were quite prepared to keep building upon that base, but the owner had a new plan (that deadly instability showing up again). When summertime arrived the station switched from its rock format to all news — a radical, 180-degree change, mind you — and it was back to square one with a different, yet equally mammoth mountain to climb. Having nowhere else to go, I stayed through the format change. (I changed my air name and went from decadent rocker to distinguished newsguy literally overnight.) But it didn't take long before I began shooting out a new batch of audition tapes.

In August of 1976 I landed at WRVQ, a CHR (Contemporary Hit Radio, or more commonly called "Top 40") station in Richmond, Virginia. Once again, I accepted a job at a station I had no prior familiarity with until I showed up for work the first day. Only this time, luck was with me.

WRVQ, or "Q94" as it's called, was the exact opposite of the Norfolk station in every way. The building, located in the historic Church Hill section of town overlooking downtown Richmond, was an opulent structure designed by the world-renowned architect Philip Johnson. (New ownership of WRVQ, and sister station WRVA, inexcusably abandoned that spectacular building as part of the consolidation craze of the 1990s, and moved the stations into some nondescript building in some nondescript part of town. Alas, that's the sort of thing that happens when the price of ones stock is held in greater regard than the condition of ones properties. An ill-fated philosophy, as history usually proves.)

Q94 was outfitted with the latest, state-of-the-art equipment. The station had a full staff of highly skilled, talented people in just about every position. It had a great on-air sound, including exciting contests and creative promotions. And it had incredible ratings — a huge listenership that put the station at or near the top of the Richmond ratings heap each time the ratings came out. In addition, Q94's owner at the time was a rock-solid company that believed in hiring and rewarding good people. Believe me, this strong, enlightened corporate culture was exactly what I needed to develop, blossom, and do exceptional work. My Norfolk-to-Richmond move was truly a 180-degree, night-to-day, life-changing experience, and all for the better.

What does this True Tale of Two Radio Stations have to do with higher prices? We're getting to that right now.

The dilapidated station in Norfolk charged next to nothing for commercial airtime. The sales department, desperate to make sales, priced 30 seconds of airtime at $1.98 or even lower. Near the end of each month when they got ever more desperate they'd reduce the price to $1, calling it "dollar a holler." No wonder this dilapidated station was dilapidated. They had no revenue and therefore no money to invest in anything. (Yes, it's a chicken-and-egg thing, where low ratings result in low prices for airtime, and low airtime prices result in low everything else.)

Contrastingly, the Richmond station charged top dollar for airtime, and kept pushing the prices ever higher. The station was a success in every aspect.

The salient point is this: The poor station with low prices was a disaster for everyone involved. It lost money for the owner. It was a demoralizing place to work, and unrewarding for employees. Since the station spent no money on the on-air product, the on-air product pretty much sucked. So it was of no benefit to listeners. And since it had no listeners, it was of no benefit to advertisers. Everyone lost.

The rich station with high prices was a success for everyone involved. It made a lot of money for the owners. Because they continually reinvested in the station, it was a delightful, rewarding place to work for the employees. And because they invested heavily in the on-air product, the station sounded terrific. Listeners loved it. And so did advertisers, who lined up to get in on the action. Businesses wanted their commercials on Q94's airwaves, and they gladly paid the rich price because of the incredible reach and tremendous results they got in return. Everyone won.

The lesson I learned first hand was that high prices, high revenue, and high profits can benefit everyone, including buyers (assuming the company reinvests a good amount of the revenue to maintain a top-quality product and exceptional service).

Caution — Dangerous Curves Ahead

As the True Tale of Two Radio Stations illustrates, everyone wins with higher prices. At least that's the way it's supposed to work. But it doesn't always work that way. Sometimes, raising your prices can result in disaster.

The truth is, raising prices is tricky business. It's like working with explosives. If you're reasonably sure what you're doing and somewhat methodical, higher prices can shoot your gross revenue and net income through the ceiling, and produce happy, loyal customers. But if you make any major mistakes, even a modest price increase can blow up in your face.

One of the more common, deadly pricing pitfalls is the *downward spiral trap.* It can happen to any business in any industry. A very visible example of it comes from the restaurant industry. I'll bet you know of a restaurant that fits into this exact transpiration:

What a wonderful place to dine, you feel. Generous helpings of great tasting food, attentive service, good prices. No wonder you and everyone else eat there regularly, and recommend it whenever you get the chance.

One day, the longtime owner decides to retire and sell out. The first month or two under the new ownership is as good as its ever been, with no visible changes.

But before long the new owner makes a painful discovery. Although the restaurant is cashflowing nicely, there isn't enough bottom-line cash available to take out what he or she wants for himself or herself each month, plus make the debt payments (having borrowed heavily to finance the purchase). In need of more cashflow each month, he or she wastes no time raising the prices and cutting expenses.

You notice the differences immediately. Your favorite entrée isn't as generous as it used to be, it isn't as succulent as it used to be, the service is slower than it used to be (they cut back on the help too), and all this costs you more. Humm . . . discontent flags are swirling around in your head. You're not so anxious to return. Everyone else notices the same declining quality and escalating prices, and they don't return as often either.

How does the new owner make up for the declining patronage and declining cashflow? Why, they administer another round of cost cuts and price increases. Which drives even more customers away.

The poor owner is sinking rapidly in the downward spiral, for which there is almost no recovery. (It would take a major infusion of new capital to regain altitude, which essentially means this new owner would be out and an even newer owner would take over.)

Remember the Primary Tenets

You may have any number of valid reasons for raising your prices. Your costs are rising, there's mounting pressure to meet expectations from the investment community, your job is on the line if you don't show better numbers this quarter, you want to finance an expansion, you're putting two kids through college, whatever. But the only valid reason to pay more in the eyes of the buyer is that he or she gets more of something in return.

Always remember Primary Tenets Number One and Number Two. Doing so will keep you going down the right road, and keep you away from most of the land mines.

Hopefully you will find this book rich in usable strategies and techniques that will enable you to earn higher prices, fatter margins, and happier customers.

Alert: Watch for Alerts

As an added bonus, I've included one or more Alerts, like this one, at the end of each chapter. They contain important implementation information. Like the warning label on a box of dynamite. We're dealing with powerful strategies here, and you need to heed the Alert warnings to come out victorious and unscathed.

Chapter One

Triple Your Price

Thought we'd start out with a pricing strategy that really rocks.

Take the price you're currently charging for your main product or service and triple it. Overnight. Starting tomorrow, the price will be three times what it is today. This is not a stunt or a fluke. Your flagship product or service is now three times the price of what it was, and it stays that way.

"You're joking, of course," I hear you rumble. While I admit this strategy sounds somewhat funny or even bizarre, I assure you I'm totally serious. Perhaps three different stories will clarify.

Story Number One — The Accountant Teaches The Marketer a Lesson

Some years ago, while attending a cocktail party, I bumped into an acquaintance I hadn't seen in three years. Recalling that the last time we spoke he had just quit his job at a major accounting firm, and along with two other CPA colleagues started his own accounting firm, I asked him how his new business was going.

"The first two years were really rough," he replied. "But the last year's been great."

"What made the last year so much better?" I asked, not really expecting any significant answer but merely carrying on conversation like one is expected to do at cocktail parties.

"We tripled our price," he said, adding "and business went through the roof."

Now my interest was piqued. Tripling ones' price to boost business is not any kind of logical or accepted business practice, I thought. If you want to increase business you lower your price, not raise it, right?

So I asked him to explain how a whopping tripling of their price could possibly result in a dramatic rise in business.

"It's very simple, Rick" he explained. "Which would you rather trust your business to — fifty-dollar-an-hour accountants that give fifty-dollar-an-hour advice, or one-hundred-and-fifty-dollar-an-hour accountants that give one-hundred-and-fifty-dollar-an-hour advice?"

"I'd want the best advice I could get," I answered.

"Exactly," he replied.

That day I learned an important lesson about the arcane nature of human behavior. I learned that a higher price can in reality be attractive to the buyer. Interesting indeed, although I didn't know what to do with this new-found revelation. I just filed it away in the back of my mind where it remained dormant until a few years later when a professional speaker friend suddenly rekindled it.

Story Number Two — The Professional Speaker Discovers the Secret

I ran into a fellow professional speaker, whom I'd known for several years, at a National Speakers Association convention a while back, and the first part of our conversation miraculously paralleled the one between myself and the accountant almost word for word. He tells me his business has exploded in the past year, I ask why, and he says it's because he tripled his speaking fee.

Of course, I asked him to explain how this could be, and he told me how he stumbled upon the secret. A prospective client, looking to hire a professional speaker to keynote their annual convention, had narrowed their selection down to three speakers, of which my friend was one. He knew the other two, and he knew their fees were considerably higher than his. So he felt pretty confident he would be the one selected.

Much to my friend's amazement and consternation, the prospect chose one of the other, more expensive speakers. Luckily, he was able to find out why. They explained it to him this way:

"This meeting is a critical one for us, and we need it to go extremely well. We really feel we need a five-thousand-dollar speaker and you're only a seventeen-hundred-dollar speaker. We went with a five-thousand-dollar speaker."

My friend ended the call, spent the rest of the day sorting it out in his mind, and decided what to do.

"I became a five-thousand-dollar speaker overnight, Rick" he told me. "And business has been rolling in ever since."

Story Number Three — The Guitar Company Turnaround

Least you think the Triple Your Price strategy only works for nebulous services that are hard to place a value on, let's talk about a physical product. Guitars, to be exact.

To relate this story, I'd like to excerpt a piece written by Eric Rhoads in his *Hello Friday* commentary. It was Eric who originally brought the story of Gibson Guitar to my attention, and he graciously allows me to include his writing here.

Those darn Japanese figured out how to dominate motorcycles, then cars, and now they were after electric guitars! A walk into any music store was evidence that the Japanese were winning yet another category.

American manufacturers were hurting, and the little Gibson Guitar Company was gasping to stay in business. The Japanese had become their worst nightmare. Gibson's product was good, but the Japanese could manufacture as good a product, import it, and sell it for less money. It didn't look like Gibson could keep making music much longer.

Legend has it that the owners of Gibson Guitar Company were drowning their sorrows with their friend Jack Daniels one night, when one of them said, "If we're going down, let's go down in style. If we've got to go under, let's go under as the most expensive guitar in America."

The next morning they tripled the price of their entire line of guitars nationwide. Over the next 60 days, as the Gibson people readied themselves for their inevitable closing, they found themselves enjoying a rash of sales — and wonderful gross profits. They were winning on price . . . the highest price.

Shoppers wondered why Gibson was three times more expensive than any other guitar. "There can only be one reason: It must be a superior guitar," buyers reasoned. Ask any guitar player today and they'll tell you that a Gibson is simply superior, and worth every penny of the price.

Not So Wacky After All

As it turns out, the Triple Your Price strategy is not all that improbable or bizarre. A number of successful companies have used it. Here's a few:

- Harley-Davidson Motorcycles experienced almost the same thing as Gibson Guitar. In the 1960s, those "darn Japanese" — specifically Honda, Yamaha, Suzuki, and Kawasaki — were coming on strong with high-quality, less expensive motorcycles. By the 1970s, Harley-Davidson was in big trouble.

    Then in the early '80s, a group of Harley-Davidson executives bought the company and devised a plan to save it. They immediately made three key moves. First, they committed to top quality. Second, they introduced some fresh new designs. And third, they tripled the prices.

    As a result, Harley-Davidson enjoys more demand than supply most of the time, has a greater market share than any competitor, and realizes a very nice profit margin. All with prices far and above the competition.

- Starbucks "gourmet" coffee cost three times more than coffee you can get at most coffee shops or restaurants. Consumers gladly pay the price and chug the product; Starbucks gladly brews the product and banks the profit.

- FedEx will deliver your letter in one or two days for around $17-$30 (depending on the distance). The United States Postal Service will deliver that same letter in one or two days for less than $9.00. Both FedEx and the USPS deliver a lot of letters, but one of them is a growing, thriving company and the other is a financial wreck most years.

- Yankee Candle prices their candles around three times more than competing brands, and they outsell competing brands by about that same margin. Isn't it interesting that in the 21st century, as we hurl through the technological revolution at warp speed, a company can succeed with an ancient, low-tech product like candles and produce outstanding revenues and profits? A candle company with the savvy to charge three times what others charge?

- A number of well-known companies successfully charge around three times more than their competitors for everyday products or services (not necessarily luxury goods). A few more examples: the Bose Wave Music System, Weber barbecue grills, Mag-Lite flashlights, Whirlpool's Duet washers and dryers, Fiskars scissors, Zippo lighters, Select Comfort's Sleep Number mattresses, Godiva chocolates, Leatherman knives, Hebrew National hot dogs, an apartment in a Trump building.

- One final example: Yours truly. I was on the phone with the owner of a speakers bureau one day several years ago, and what a red-letter day this turned out to be.* His agency was having a hard time booking me for speeches, and the reason he gave about caused me to fall out of my chair. He said I was just too darn cheap. His clients, major corporations and associations,

---

*Speakers bureaus act as booking agents for professional speakers.

hired major-league speakers, and my low fee kept me out of that category. He suggested a fee I should charge, and guess what? The figure he mentioned just happened to be three times what I had been charging.

This conversation took place on a Friday afternoon. By the start of business Monday morning, my fee had tripled. And sure enough, it worked like a charm. Much more business at a much higher price. Is this a great country or what?

Welcome to the Major Leagues

I know what you're thinking.

"My customers squawk if I raise my price only five percent. They'd never accept even a twenty percent increase, let alone a two-hundred percent increase!"

You're right. Your current customers probably won't accept a 200-percent price increase. But a whole new slate of customers just might.

Remember my accountant friend who tripled his fees? Know what happened to his customers when they heard about the increase? They took their business elsewhere. But a whole new crop of customers came on board. Bigger, better clients who could not only afford the higher fees but expected to, and were accustomed to, paying accountants in that higher range.

In other words, the accountant replaced his $50-an-hour clients with $150-an-hour clients.

"We moved up to the major leagues," as he put it.

Same thing happened to the professional speaker when he tripled his fee. The people who had been hiring him could no longer afford him. But with the higher fee, he became credible, desirable to a different segment of the market (much larger organizations with much larger budgets).

When Gibson Guitar tripled their prices, aspiring guitarists could no longer afford them. But established, successful musicians now began buying Gibsons. Gibson became the brand of guitar that successful musicians owned and budding musicians dreamed of owning.

When you Triple Your Price, you are saying goodbye to your existing customers and saying hello to a whole new segment of the marketplace. You're pricing yourself out of one market and into another. You're entering the main arena, stepping into the big leagues. You are now courting a segment of the market that wants to pay more, expects to pay more, and has the budget in place to pay more. Sounds enticing, doesn't it?

The Magic is in Tripling

Why is it a tripling of the price? Why not doubling or quadrupling? Why not a simple five percent rise?

If you only raise your prices by a modest amount, say four or five percent, you're still in the same arena. You will still invite price comparison, and you'll be seen as merely a higher-priced version of the same thing. But when you triple your price, you're catapulting yourself out of that arena entirely and into a whole new arena — one in which you may occupy all by yourself, or with much fewer, élite competitors.

There's also a mystical, magical, otherwise unexplainable force that you tap into when you triple your price. Doubling, quadrupling, or anything else just doesn't do it. The magic is in tripling.

One more point of clarification. This strategy calls for you to triple your price. That may land you priced side-by-side with a whole new set of competitors or it may land you priced three times more than your nearest competitor. Either works. Just be sure you triple your price (assuming you choose to implement this strategy), then operate from wherever that puts you relative to the competition.

(You can raise your prices by a modest amount, say five percent or so, using other strategies in this book. But if you're going to use the Triple Your Price strategy, it must indeed be a tripling.)

Are You Ready to Triple Your Price?

The good news is that the Triple Your Price strategy has the potential to catapult your revenues quickly and dramatically. The bad news is that this strategy is not for everyone. You have to have a special set of qualifications in place for it to work. Specifically, you need these three prerequisites:

1. **You must have a top quality product or service.** When you triple your price, you're making a statement. You're declaring your product and/or service to be far and away the best, or in the top echelon. And it had better be. If you're not noticeably better, the marketplace will knock you back down almost immediately.

2. **You have to look like the best.** Appearance counts. In fact, it rules. You may need a major image makeover to justify your newer, higher price.

    When the accountants tripled their fees, they moved from Class B office space to Class A office space in the most prestigious high rise in town.

My professional speaker friend replaced his computer-printed brochures with professionally-printed, full color brochures on expensive paper. He also had new, better photos taken and did a major upgrade to his web site.

Before announcing my new higher fees to the marketplace, I upgraded. All new, fancier sales materials, higher-class wardrobe, snazzier car. (As superficial, shallow, and disgusting as it may be, the fact remains that we are all judged by our appearance, which includes the car we drive.)

3. **You must have the courage to do it and not look back.** Let's face it, tripling ones' prices and waiving goodbye to ones' current customers does take a good amount of guts, moxie, chutzpah, cajones.

Interestingly, it helps if you're not doing particularly well right now. Think about Gibson Guitar. They were sinking rapidly and on the verge of bankruptcy. Tripling their price didn't seem like such a risky move when they had nothing to lose. Conversely, if your business — or a particular product or service — is doing real well now, you're probably not a good candidate for the Triple Your Price strategy.

Alert: Announce Your Price Increase 90 Days in Advance to Your Existing Customers.

I stated earlier that when you triple your price you have to be willing to abandon your current customers who most likely won't be willing or able to afford you anymore. But I didn't say you should leave them feeling burnt, angry, or vengeful.

If you have long-standing relationships with your customers, from a practical or respectful standpoint, you should let them know of your plans well in advance, and help them find another supplier if need be. Explain that your dramatic price increases are due to a fundamental shift in the direction of your business, not any kind of attempt to gouge them. The reaction you want from your current customer is not "Why you dirty #@%&*#! How could you do this to me?!" Rather, you're going for a reaction along this line: "I understand. You're going after a different segment of the market. I'm probably too small for you. Good luck, and let me know if I can help."

Alert: Plan for Long Term Success.

When you have an ultra high price, it will probably work well for you eight out of ten years. But every decade or so, when the economy tightens, you may experience a sudden drop in business. If you're smart, you understand and expect this short-term aberration. You've planned for it financially and otherwise. You maintain your pricing position. On the other hand, there have been managers who panic when revenues slow down and abandon their lofty price position, only to end up demolishing the whole thing they had so adroitly built over the preceding years.

Chapter Two

Create a
Great Customer Experience

You've heard it said several times before, I'm sure. There's no magic formula. No silver bullet. No wonder elixir. No sure-fire method that guarantees success in business.

Well, I'm not so sure about that. Turns out there is a magic formula and it does get you as close to guaranteed success as possible. It's called the Great Customer Experience, or Greater Customer Experience, compared to what you used to have or to the norm in your industry. It's underlying logic couldn't be simpler.

Like water that always seeks its own level, buyers will naturally gravitate to the most pleasurable buying experience. Customers innately seek to feel joy, confidence, acceptance, piece of mind, or any other pleasurable emotion, when buying. The company that provides the most pleasure (and avoids the most displeasures) wins the most business. Virtually every time.*

---

*The only thing that can negate the effectiveness of the Great Customer Experience is inept management, which can ruin even the best of businesses.

Which Convenience Store Do You Prefer?

Here's an example of the greater customer experience, and how it naturally attracts customers.

7-Eleven is the grandaddy of convenience stores. They've been around forever it seems (since 1927 to be exact), with practically the same building design, interior layout, and product selection. Other than a few tough periods over the decades, which is not unusual for a company that's been around this long, 7-Eleven is a successful, profitable business.

As you would expect in our competitive, free-enterprise society, there are other convenience store chains spreading across the country. Sheetz is one, Wawa another. (Sheetz and Wawa are both based in Pennsylvania. An interesting coincidence, albeit irrelevant to this discussion.)

A new Sheetz store recently opened about a mile from my house. The first thing I noticed is the large, brightly lit parking area with easy in-and-out access. Much bigger and better than the typical 7-Eleven's cramped, dimly-lit parking area. The second thing I noticed is the twelve gas pumps at the Sheetz, compared to 7-Eleven's four.

And that's just the outside. Upon entering the Sheetz I see a contemporary designed, colorful, fun decor. Neat and clean. Friendly, energetic personnel. And my favorite: made-to-order fast food that tastes pretty darn good. I simply touch a computer screen to custom order my club sub, and a real live human being makes it on the spot in a couple minutes.

Compared to 7-Eleven, Sheetz is by far the Greater Customer Experience. No wonder Sheetz, along with Wawa (which has an equally good customer experience) are growing so quickly.

I'm not suggesting 7-Eleven make wholesale changes and be-come a Sheetz-like clone. They have, after all, a tried-and-true for-mula that works for them. I merely make the observation that when a Sheetz or Wawa is located within a mile or less of a 7-Eleven, the dozen or so vehicles buzzing in and out of the Sheetz or Wawa greatly outnumber the two or three cars doing likewise at the 7-Eleven, on a typical afternoon. It would appear consumers recog-nize a Greater Customer Experience when they encounter one, and choose it over the lesser customer experience.

It's the Buying Experience

One key factor that affects the prices you're able to charge is the quality of your product and/or service. In the previous chapter I mentioned that you need a top-quality product or service to make the Triple Your Price strategy work, and the same is true for the Create a Great Customer Experience strategy. In fact, you'll need a high quality product and/or service to make almost every strategy in this book work.

Therefore we'll assume that you do have a high quality prod-uct and/or service. I won't mention it too much any more. Instead, we'll focus on other factors that affect the prices you can charge.

When I say you need to create a greater customer experience, I'm speaking mainly about the buying experience itself, which is what the customer feels or experiences while they are in the process of investigating, deciding, and buying. Included in the buying experi-ence is after-the-sale support as well.

So, we'll define the greater customer experience as something that deals mainly with the buying and support functions. We'll focus on what the customer encounters, undergos, and feels while they are in the process of buying from you and accessing the support you offer.

The Greater Customer Experience in Action

Let's look at a few examples of the Great Customer Experience, or GCE, in a variety of industries.

• In their book *Built From Scratch,* the co-founders of The Home Depot, Bernie Marcus and Arthur Blank, explained the importance of creating an exciting, fun atmosphere inside their stores. They also wanted to establish a level of service so high that no customer would ever leave a Home Depot store unhappy. Other successful retailers, especially high-priced ones, have similar objectives.

By the way, have you ever noticed that with successful retailers, whether as large as The Home Depot or as small as a mom-and-pop store, good managers spend a great deal of their time on the sales floor involved in the action? Conversely, managers of struggling retail businesses tend to spend most of their time hiding in the back room instead of working the floor. If you're a retailer, and you want to create a greater customer experience, get your managers out of the shadows and onto the floor as much as possible. This goes for senior executives, too, who should maintain a direct connection with what's going on in their stores.

Some people have criticized The Home Depot for putting a slew of small hardware stores and other home supply stores out of business in whatever town Home Depot enters. (Walmart has encountered similar negative sentiment upon occasion.) Yet such thinking simply doesn't hold up to objective reality. The verity of it all is that the marketplace, which is the collective choice of numerous individuals, determines which businesses succeed and which businesses fail. As I said, consumers will naturally gravitate to the greater customer experience. If those oldline, dusty, dingy, crusty hardware stores are outmatched by a greater customer experience somewhere else, they should expect to lose business.

• Jeff Bezos, the founder and CEO of Amazon.com, often talks about the importance of creating a great customer experience. Sure enough, Amazon does have the most compelling and buyer-friendly experience on the internet, not to mention mechanically the easiest and fastest site to navigate.

• For State Farm Insurance, the GCE is achieved in part by having their offices located close to their customers, in residential neighborhoods rather than in distant office towers. When a State Farm policy holder has a claim, they call the same person that sold them the insurance, not who-knows-who, who-knows-where. State Farm believes that their clients get a greater customer experience, including a higher level of confidence and security, when they maintain a "good neighbor" relationship between salesperson and client.

• Apple established their own brick-and-mortar stores because they found it nearly impossible to have a great customer experience without controlling the customer experience themselves. So the Apple stores are roomy, clean, elegant. The products are displayed on waist-high tables, and they're running. You can walk up to any product and test-drive it on the spot. They have knowledgeable salespeople, including a Genius Bar where any question or problem can be handled. No wonder the Apple stores have been hugely successful. The GCE wins every time.

• Contrary to the old, shifty "used car salesman" image, I've found that most modern auto dealerships actually have a pretty good customer experience. Even so, there's always room to improve. CarMax has done exactly that, creating a GCE by taking the biggest negatives of used cars — low inventory, questionable quality, high-pressure salespeople, price haggling — and totally reversing them. CarMax's biggest selling points are huge inventory, high quality used cars, no-pressure salespeople, and a no-haggle, set price.

• FedEx is truly a GCE creator and innovator. There is no easier, more hassle-free way to arrange a shipment than to contact FedEx. And no more trustworthy way of assuring delivery than using FedEx's tracking system. UPS has an equally good GCE. Seems a great customer experience will work for every business, even arch rivals.

• Some savvy retailers are promoting their GCE with the clever use of slogans. Kohl's has used the slogan "Shop happy, leave happy." Best Buy has used the slogan "Turn on the fun." Publix, the dominant supermarket chain in the southeast, has used the slogan "Where shopping is a pleasure."

Notice that each slogan refers to the buying experience, which is, as pointed out earlier, where the GCE lies.

The Secret is the Details

One of the truly remarkable greater customer experiences can be found at Wegman's supermarket. Listing the many attributes of their GCE would require more space than available, so let me see what I can do with a few short paragraphs.

Wegman's is so clean you could eat off the floor. No wonder — the employees are constantly cleaning and tidying. There's a Café inside, where you can have a hot meal, smorgasbord style. Chicken wings, pizza, and yes, sushi. All fresh, made on the spot. The salad bar is large, extravagant, and kept constantly fresh. There's also a complete restaurant and bar inside with a full menu of really good dishes.

Wegman's also has prepared fresh food meals. Take one home, heat it up, and enjoy home cooking the easy way. Although product quality is outside our definition of the GCE, I'm mentioning it to give you a big-picture idea of what Wegman's is all about.

Back to the service. Here's what happened to me at a Wegman's recently. In the checkout lane, as I was picking my items out of the cart and placing them on the conveyor belt, a sandwich container busted open and the sandwich tumbled out onto the conveyor belt and bounced onto the floor. Immediately . . . and by that I mean within a few seconds . . . a manager appeared, radioed to someone, and that someone came trotting up with an exact replacement sandwich. And the manager apologized for the inconvenience, which really wasn't necessary because I wasn't inconvenienced at all. Actually, I noted how fast and efficiently they fixed this little mishap.

A few years ago I happened to mention how great Wegman's is to my sister. She does not live in a part of the country with a Wegman's store and has never been to one.

"So, what's the one big thing that makes Wegman's so great?" she asked. I stopped to think, then said "It isn't one big thing. It's a thousand small things."

Herein lies the real secret of the great customer experience. It's not any one thing but an amalgamation of numerous detailed things.

If you're going to create and maintain a great customer experience, you must be a detail-oriented thinker. Or if you're not, then you have to hire detail-oriented people and let them know you revere detailed thinking, and that you reward detailed execution.

Creating and maintaining a great customer experience is like working out to maintain a lean, muscular, sculpted body. It takes work. But once you get in the habit, it becomes a way of life and the effort comes naturally. You may even become hooked on it, feeling your own jolt of excitement every time you discover or implement yet another way the customer is delightfully served during purchase and support.

Think Time and Senses

If we microscopically dissect the great customer experience, we see that's it's all about time and senses.

People are pressed for time, and they're looking for any possible way to save hours, minutes, seconds. With the exception of retirees, consumers value their time more than their money. Which means they will pay money to save time. When creating your GCE, think of ways you can save the buyer time. Innovate. Invent. If it saves the client time, it's probably a good idea.

At one time I co-owned a direct mail marketing company. We created proprietary direct mail campaigns and sold them to businesses across the country. We printed and mailed tens of millions of pieces each year.

Since our company didn't own a printing plant, we subcontracted out all the printing. Good business sense dictates you buy from a variety of vendors, to not only keep competition among them alive, but to minimize your risk in case any one vendor goes under or experiences any other production problems. Yet we ended up buying all the printing from only one printer. Oh, we tried spreading the business around, but all these other printers couldn't seem to grasp what we needed. And what we needed was speed. Not necessarily printing speed, but rather information speed.

Our clients tended to become rather nervous about these expensive projects. They'd call us day and night with questions like "How many have you printed today?", "Are they in the mail yet?," and "When will they be hitting mailboxes?" We had to have accurate answers for them, and we had to have it whenever they called.

Printing salespeople tend to function in a slow-paced world, or at least they act that way. They never understood what "need the answer right away" meant. They acted as though "right away" meant they could call back a day or two later. One printing salesperson did get it, however. Whenever we called him with a production question, day, night, or on the weekends, he'd call us back within an hour or less with the information we needed (which we were then able to pass along to our clients). He understood that we needed up-to-the-minute information immediately, and he acted accordingly. As a consequence, he got all the business. At whatever the price.

We all experience things through our five senses. Therefore, the great customer experience is really a sensory experience. It's through the buyer's own eyes, ears, nose, mouth, or hands that they're going to experience what you're all about.

When creating your CGE, think of ways to improve what they see, hear, smell, taste, or feel. Take them one at a time, and ask yourself and your management team these two questions: "During the buying or support experience, what does the customer see (or hear, smell, taste, feel)?" And "What should the customer see (or hear, smell, taste, feel) that would make their buying and support experience better?"

Suspend Your Own Managerial Experience

Managerial experience in any particular line of work is certainly a valuable asset. It's 95 percent good. But the bad part about experience is that the more experienced you are, the more close-minded you become to different ways of doing things. Yet to create a greater customer experience, you have to be open to new, different, better ways of doing things.

Isn't it interesting that most innovation comes from outside the industry in question? Fred Smith had not been in the package delivery business before he founded FedEx. Jeff Bezos had not been in the book selling business until he founded Amazon. The personal computer wasn't invented by IBM or Honeywell or Sperry Rand or Burroughes or any of the big mainframe companies of the day.

It was invented by two college-age guys in a garage (of course, I'm referring to Steve Jobs and Steve Wozniak, the founders of Apple Computer). British entrepreneur Richard Branson named his company Virgin because every new venture he undertakes (and he's in and out of a lot of them) is in an industry he's never been in before. He usually comes up with new ways of doing things in each case. Some of these new ideas don't pan out. No one bats 1,000. But you will greatly increase the odds of doing things right when you do them with the greater customer experience in mind.

Notice the wave of young people creating industry-disrupting companies? In almost every case, they establish a greater customer experience as part of their disruption business model. Without that GCE component, a disruption isn't likely to work, I do believe.

Assume the Buyer's Position

What specific things should you do to create a greater customer experience? That's very easy to determine if you take the buyer's perspective. Buyers could probably rattle off a list of things you could do better without hesitation. They see the good and bad instantly. Whereas we, who are so ingrained in our particular businesses, can't see it most of the time.

I'll bet you and I could visit each other's businesses and within one hour have a list of at least ten things the other could do to improve the buying or support experience. What would happen if you and three or four of your counterparts at different businesses in different industries met and examined one another's businesses, looking for ways to improve the customer experience? I'm sure you'd have no trouble coming up with specific ways the others could improve, and they'd plop a similar list on your lap.

Let's Talk Money

By now you're probably saying "But I can't afford to institute all kinds of wondrous things to improve the customer experience. It would require too much up-front investment, and be too costly to maintain." In response, let me make three important points.

1. There's no faster ROI.

The main reason your business exists is to deliver something consumers want or need (that is, after all, where the money comes from). And the second main reason you're in business is to make money and produce a good return on investment for the owner(s), wouldn't you say? And the faster that return on investment comes in, the better, right?

Well, it's my observation that nothing contributes to a faster return on investment than the great customer experience. That's because buyers see it immediately and respond to it immediately. They quickly become repeat customers. With a great customer experience, you win business right away, every day. Your ROI is looking better and better, in direct proportion to your GCE.

2. It's the cheapest form of advertising.

The best way to get word-of-mouth spreading is with a great customer experience. Not only do customers talk favorably about you and recommend you, they bring other customers back with them.

In addition, with a great customer experience in effect, you may be able to cut back on your advertising. When a new Sheetz or Wawa open, they're packed from day one. And that's with a minimal amount of advertising, if any. The greater customer experience is a powerful buyer magnet, requiring less media-purchased persuasion (assuming potential customers are aware of you and your product or service).

3. You can raise your prices and attract more business.

The biggest point of all: The greater customer experience allows you to raise your prices, fatten your margins, and simultaneously attract more business.

FedEx and UPS are around five to ten times more expensive than the United States Postal Service, depending on the particular service in question. If price were the issue, FedEx and UPS would be struggling and the USPS would be thriving. Yet it's the other way around. The GCE wins, even with the higher price.

Wegman's is not the cheapest grocery store. Neither is Whole Foods or Publix, which are probably the highest-priced grocery chains you'll encounter. Yet Whole Foods, Wegmans, and Publix do very well, despite competition from the nation's biggest chains, including Kroger, Walmart, Aldi, and Food Lion, which tend to compete on price.

Disneyland and Disneyworld are high priced in just about every aspect. They also have a great customer experience. Does the high price keep people from experiencing the fun, excitement, cleanliness, and exceptional customer service of Disney's parks? Not hardly.

With the greater customer experience, you can negate price

issues. People gravitate to the GCE, and they're willing to pay for it.

Alert: Reconcile Change and Stability.

Creating a greater customer experience inherently involves frequent change in the ways you sell or support. If these changes improve or enhance the buyer's experience (which is what's supposed to happen), this type of change is good for your business.

On the other hand, managerial stability is a solid asset. The things you don't want to change very often, if at all, are your values and philosophies (assuming they've proven successful for you in the past). Strong companies are built upon a solid foundation of values and philosophies which can stand up to the rotating ravages of the business world.

Chapter Three

Adopt Xahgoh Pricing

There exists an overwhelmingly pervasive pricing technique, loosely called *psychological pricing*, that I'm sure you're familiar with. It goes like this: For an item with a market value of $1.00, you price it at 99 cents. An item with a market value of $20.00 is priced at $19.95. An item with a $400.00 market value is priced at $399.99. You get the idea.

The underlying theory is that $399.99 will somehow seem significantly lower — and therefore more attractive — to the buyer than $400.00. Which translates into more sales at the one-cent-lower price.

"I'd really like to own that nice looking lawnmower, but the four-hundred dollar price is just too expensive. But at three-hundred ninety-nine dollars and ninety-nine cents it's a steal and I'm buyin'!" Sounds kind of silly, yet this is the general notion of how psychological pricing is supposed to work.

This kind of reasoning can be taken to an extreme. Some marketers, for example, believe that a one-tenth-of-a-cent price drop has the same effect as an entire cent drop. Why price something at $2.99 when you can achieve the same result (increased sales) at $2.99.9? You're still using psychological pricing, but it's only costing you one-tenth of a cent (as opposed to an entire cent) to do it, they reason.

Check the gas pump the next time you fill up. Gasoline is priced in tenths of cents, in case you had forgotten. Gas pump manufacturers even build the pumps to operate this way, as though no gas retailer would ever want to do it differently. Do you really think consumers buy more gas because a gallon is priced one-tenth of a cent less? Most vehicle tanks only hold but so much gas — once you fill up you can't buy more even if that one-tenth-of-a-cent lower price somehow injected your brain with insatiable desire.

The Truth Comes Out

Would it interest you to know that there has never been any evidence, scientific study or otherwise, that supports the notion that psychological pricing actually works? That more sales are made at $2.95 than at $3? Or at $99.99 than at $100?

If there's no proof that psychological pricing works, why do so many marketers use it? Probably because we've become so used to it we simply accept it as the "correct" method of pricing (there must be some wisdom behind it somewhere, right?). And because no one's ever questioned it, or offered any other pricing method as an alternative. Until now.

Good Digits and Bad Digits

Let me introduce you to a whole new method of pricing your products or services called *Xahgoh pricing* (pronounced Zāy'-gō). It recognizes and utilizes the subatomic magnetic power of each digit. There are, as it turns out, inherently "attractive digits" that subconsciously activate a positive brain response, and there are inherently "repellent digits" that subconsciously activate a negative brain response. There are also "neutral digits" that don't activate much brain response either way.

In no particular order . . .

- The attractive digits are: 2, 3, 7.
- The repellent digits are: 5, 8, 9.
- The neutral digits are: 1, 4, 6.
- The wild-card digit is 0. Zero can be attractive, repellent, or neutral, depending on how it's used. More on this later.

Converting to Xahgoh

Pricing your products or services with the Xahgoh method is simply a matter of using the attractive digits whenever possible, using the neutral digits as your second choice, and avoiding use of the repellent digits unless absolutely necessary.

For example, that lawnmower psychologically priced at $399.99 can be Xahgoh priced at, say, $377.77. In this case we've replaced all those dastardly nines with alluring sevens.

However, you may have noticed that in this particular conversion to Xahgoh pricing, we ended up lowering the price. While it may be desirable to lower a price at certain times, doing so is not in keeping with the theme of this book. The objective is to find ways to raise your prices — ways that actually result in more sales at higher margins. And let me tell you, Xahgoh is an absolutely wonderful way to do exactly that.

So instead of converting our $399.99 lawnmower to $377.77, why not convert it to $411.37? It's Xahgoed and it's higher. Two bangs for no buck. (Using Xahgoh pricing costs you nothing, I point out.)

Xahgohing Drink Prices

A restaurant I was advising had a minor dilemma, or so the regional VP believed. He felt they needed to raise their drink prices, but he was afraid a price increase would turn off their loyal customers and impede sales. When I suggested there was a way they could raise their drink prices and simultaneously stimulate sales, his reluctance suddenly turned to anxiousness, as you can imagine.

It was simply a matter of converting from psychological pricing to Xahgoh pricing, and raising the prices in the process. Specifically, here's what we did:

- The small size drink went from 89 cents to $1 even.
- The medium size drink went from 99 cents to $1.12.
- The large size drink went from $1.19 to $1.37.

As a result, drink sales did indeed increase. And get this: *no one noticed the price increase.* At least no customer mentioned it or reacted negatively to it. With Xahgoh pricing you get yet another benefit: Price increases tend to go unnoticed.

"We did a stealth price increase!" the restaurant VP exclaimed. I guess so.

Price increases, using Xahgoh's attractive digits, tend to go unrecognized because people don't remember the attractive digits as well as they remember the repellent digits. The brain tends to consciously ignore a positive or neutral stimulus more so than a negative stimulus. Nine people can walk into a room and you'll not consciously notice that they all smell good, but that tenth person who forgot to use deodorant can send you scurrying away. The negative stimulus caused your brain to kick the matter into conscious attention. The same thing happens when you perceive that song you hate continually popping up on the radio or streaming service. Because it's a negative stimulator for you, you're more aware of it.

When you use the attractive digits of 2, 3, and 7, consumers are less aware of it.

The Wild Zero

The zero can be attractive, repellent, or neutral, depending on how you use it.

There are two variables that dictate how the zero should be used. The first is ticket size, and the second is decimal direction.

We'll define a small-ticket item as something priced under $1,000, and a big-ticket item as something priced at $1,000 or above.

For small-ticket items, left of the decimal point: the zero is repellent and should be avoided. Examples of $10.00, $307.33, and $690.99 have the danger light blinking. $11.00, $327.33, and $712.31 are possible improvements.

For small-ticket items, right of the decimal point (the cents area): the zero is neutral. Therefore $11.00 is okay, although $11.30 is better since attractive digits are more desirable than neutral digits.

For big-ticket items, left of the decimal point: the zero is attractive. Thus $1,000, $6,700, and $200,000 are all good.

The zero can be used to indicate the price of a big-ticket item is rounded off and not precise, which is sometimes desirable. For example, if you're submitting a bid for some kind of contract service, landscape maintenance let's say, you wouldn't want to price it at $77,322.37, even though all the digits are attractive. The problem with this is, it implies you've precisely calculated every cent or dollar, which opens the door for debate about each component cost. ("If we drop the third application of fertilizer, can we save six thousand, three-hundred twenty-two dollars and fourteen cents?" the prospect inquires.) In this example, a price of $77,300 is much better. The sevens and threes are attractive, as are the judiciously used zeros.

For big-ticket items, right of the decimal point: the zero is repellent. Therefore $1,200.00, $6,700.07, and $200,000.30 are not good. The solution, for a big-ticket item, is to simply drop the cents altogether.

Cents and Decimal are Optional

Whether big-ticket or small-ticket, there's nothing wrong with pricing something at even dollar amounts if you don't think cents will work to your advantage. Our restaurant example, with the small drink priced at $1, is a case in point. Some discount retailers, known generically as "dollar stores," price things in even dollar amounts and that is a sound concept.

When you do price something at an even dollar amount, you have the option of showing the zeros after the decimal point or not showing the zeros after the decimal point. Thus $1.00, $17.00, and $477.00 are good, as are $1 or $17 or $477. In this case, even showing the decimal point is optional. In the last three examples, the after-decimal zeros and the decimal point itself are implied, but not shown.

If you sell impulse items at high-traffic events, such as food and drink at the fair, souvenirs at sporting events, or even lemonade on the street corner, you'll be better off pricing in even dollars and dropping cents from your sale price. Speed is the key to large sales at hectic, high-traffic events. Customers are throwing bills down, grabbing the items, and moving on. They haven't got the time to fumble with coinage or wait for you to make change.

You don't even have to charge a sales tax if you don't want to. There is no law anywhere that requires you to collect sales tax from buyers. There are laws, however, that require you to *pay* sales or use tax to the state and local community in which your business is domiciled or in which the sales take place. With regard to fast sales at hectic events, you'll usually come out ahead by pricing your items without sales tax added on, and then paying the sales tax out of your gross revenue.

Double Digiting

The three attractive digits — 2, 3, and 7 (and 0 when used in its attractive manner) — tend to increase in potency when each is used twice (or in the case of zero, three times) in a row. Examples are $22, $33, $14.77, $341.22 and $77,000.

Also, the three neutral digits — 1, 4, and 6 — can be biased slightly toward the attractive by double digiting, although not enough to recatagorize them as attractive digits.

The three repellent digits — 5, 8, and 9 — also increase in potency by double digiting, but in the negative direction. Double-digiting the repellent digits is the worst possible pricing structure.

Beyond Pricing

You can use the subconscious attractiveness of digits 2, 3, and 7 outside the realm of pricing, if the opportunity arises. Used correctly, the numbers 2, 3, and 7 can strengthen persuasion and weaken opposing argument. (Conversely, you would want to avoid use of the three repellent digits in such instances.)

Use the number 2 when describing courses of action, directions, schools of thought, or opposing philosophies. Example: "There are two different roads we could go down. One would eventually lead to failure, the other to success."

Use the number 3 when listing points, steps, or components. Example: "I see three main challenges. First, we need to [bla-bla], secondly we need to [bla-bla], and finally we must [bla-bla]."

Use the number 7 when establishing something of lasting significance or permanence. Examples might include your list of corporate values, your number of divisions or profit centers, or the number of sections in your proposal. (Make sure there are seven of each.)

The Origin of Xahgoh

You may be curious as to where Xahgoh pricing comes from. Its origin dates back to antiquity, when Asian shipping merchants collaborated with vagabond Zenists on the lost continent of Tipalia during the Earth's first recorded polarization reversal.

Just kidding. Actually, you may have to come up with some explanation when someone questions your use of it. If you can't think of anything better, feel free to use the one I just provided.

Meanwhile, here's the real story. Over the years, I became aware of several different businesses in different industries using different aspects of what eventually became Xahgoh pricing. I found evidence of its partial use in retail (especially with the pricing of impulse items), evidence of its partial use in direct marketing, and evidence of its partial use in the arts, of all places. Each user of one aspect of it — favoring the number three, as just one example — was apparently unaware of the existence of other parts — the avoidance of the number nine, as another example.

I concluded it would be helpful to marketers if all those bits and pieces were collected and organized into one cohesive system. I gathered the parts and began assembling, exercising caution so as not to let it become too complex or unwieldy. It needed to remain simple and usable.

I also decided this newly assembled technique should have a unique name, so as to aid communication of it. I christened it Xahgoh, heretofore a nonsense word with no other discernible meaning.

Finally, I apologize to the confirmed numerologist whose territory I may have unintentionally but unavoidably stepped on. Let me assure you, the practice of numerology, for whatever it's worth, remains fully intact, despite Xahgoh's prance through.

Subconscious Benefit is Valid Benefit

Primary Tenet Number One, you'll recall, states that if it doesn't benefit the buyer, it won't work. Just how does Xahgoh pricing benefit the buyer?

First off, Xahgoh seems more straightforward, or "honest" if you will, than psychological pricing, which attempts to create a lower-price illusion by knocking off an inconsequential five cents or one cent or even one-tenth of a cent (ie: $39.99 instead of $40.00). With Xahgoh, there is no attempt to bend perception.

Most importantly, Xahgoh pricing does a good job of giving the consumer what he or she really wants. Assuming the theory of Xahgoh is valid — that most people find the numbers 2, 3, and 7 more appealing than 5, 8, and 9 — then we are catering to that desire when we price things using 2s, 3s, and 7s. Consciously and logically, the buyer may acknowledge no special affinity for the attractive digits of 2, 3, and 7, and may in fact, denounce such notion. But it is not the conscious, logical mind we are appealing to when we Xahgoh price. It is the subconscious mind we are accommodating, which is the part of the mind that controls most of our behavior. It goes back to the old truism that what people say they do and what they actually do are often two different things. Xahgoh pricing deals with what people actually do, based on subconscious desire, which is just as valid as conscious desire.

Alert: It May Just Work for You.

I said at the outset that there is no credible evidence that the antiquated psychological pricing actually works. Well, there's no similar evidence that Xahgoh pricing works either (except for the occasional anecdotal). But, you've got to price your products and services in some manner, according to some reasonable method, so why not give Xahgoh a try?

If you do experience quantifiable results, or should decide to undertake some sort of scientific study of the matter, be sure and inform us of the results.

Chapter Four

Project Status and Prestige

Status and prestige. A duet of emotional feelings so powerful they make royalty out of commoners, champs out of chumps, and stars out of no one. Or so it seems in the mind of the beholder.

Status and prestige are similar in that they are both exhilarating emotions that result in feelings of importance, superiority, or success. For purposes of this discussion, we'll treat status and prestige as one entity, and even refer to them collectively as S&P once in a while for short.

Humans innately and subconsciously crave S&P, and will pay handsomely for it. If you market a product or service in such a manner as to project a good amount of status and prestige, you greatly strengthen your ability to raise your prices and attract more business.

Who or What We Associate With

Assuming you choose to implement this strategy, your product, service, or business — combined with its marketing — needs to exude some amount of status and prestige. The consumer then buys, instinctively believing that the status and prestige you project will subsequently rub off or transfer to them, resulting in an enhancement in their own personal level of status and prestige.

Put another way: People want to associate with something or someone that exudes a high level of status and prestige because doing so raises their own level of status and prestige. Associating is the key.

Associating with someone or something that projects status and prestige is a subconscious desire. People don't logically think about it nor do they question it. They just do it. They'll scramble to get their picture taken with a celebrity at some meet and greet, tell stories about the time they bumped into so-and-so (someone in the news), or purchase and wear designer sunglasses or jeans. Given a choice they'll ride in the more expensive car, attend the more ostentatious party, or join the most exclusive country club.

Some people even overdose on status and prestige. Stories abound of high-living people who suddenly turn up broke, their addiction to the high of status and prestige leading to their downfall, or at least contributing measurably to it. Others fabricate stories or eyewitness testimony to get the sudden taste of attention and importance they've craved and have found otherwise elusive, only to die in shame when the truth finally comes out. And others will suddenly abandon home, family, and career to spend a few months or years frolicking in the presence of some psuedo-celebrity or guru who has mesmerized them with a taste of higher status and prestige.

Like a powerful drug, high doses of S&P can be addictive and destructive. While we marketers certainly don't want to dispense anything that is harmful to the consumer, we do want to acknowledge the important role S&P plays in affecting purchase decisions, and see if we can utilize that to everyone's benefit.

Price is a Great Status and Prestige Projector

Great luck! Price and S&P are directly related. The higher the price, the higher the level of S&P. (Other variables can negate this, but for now, let's assume nothing is negating it.)

You know how this works. A $65,000 car exudes more status than a $24,000 car. An $800,000 house exudes more prestige than a $250,000 house. And that $250,000 house exudes more S&P than a $150,000 house. A $130 pair of shoes exudes more bling-bling (one of the more whimsical slang terms for raw S&P) than a $24.00 pair of shoes.

So, let's reason along: If people innately want status and prestige, and a high price contributes to that, then people want to pay a high price.

Of course, none of us will admit we want to pay a lot of money for something, or that we are seeking higher status. That's the conscious, logical mind speaking. But subconsciously, when status and prestige are to be gained, we gladly spend, spend, spend.

Your Author Spends a Lot of Money and Gets Valuable S&P

I'll admit straight out that I sometimes spend big bucks to get an S&P rush. I can tell you this with certainty: When I'm wearing an Armani suit, custom made dress shirt, Richel tie, and gold-plated Parker pen (my personal favorite), I feel like I'm ready to conquer the world. My performance really is enhanced. The S&P I receive, and the results I get, make these high-priced items worth every dollar.

Could I feel the same high level of S&P with less expensive accoutrement? Well, there was a time when yours truly could be seen wearing a no-name polyester suit, discount shirt, and garage-sale tie. At least I owned a suit, which was more than many of us sophomoric dandies did back in the eighties. But my level of performance was commensurate with this dreadful ensemble. A relatively low level, as I recall.

Status and prestige are powerful emotions that can result in noticeable, measurable performance improvement. The mental equivalent of an energy drink or performance-enhancing drug. Paying a high price for something — and experiencing the motivating jolt of status and prestige — is a much better feeling than paying a low price for something and feeling nothing but the weather, let me tell you.

They Buy Neither the Drill Nor the Hole

There's an old marketing adage that says people don't buy the drill, they buy the hole. Meaning the buyer is concerned with the end result, not how that result happened. But if this were true, why would anyone buy a Makita drill for $100 instead of a Skil drill for $43? They both make the same round, nice-looking hole.

If buyers were only concerned with the end result, why would they purchase a Lexus instead of a Chevrolet? Or a Lotus instead of a Lexus? Just about any make of automobile will get you from point A to point B. Consumers want the end result, no question. But they also want — and will pay dearly for — the status and prestige they feel in the process.

Not Exclusive to Luxury

Don't think that status and prestige are reserved strictly for luxury goods accessible to only the rich and famous. Practically any product, service, or business, at any level, can make good use of S&P. Even lowly street gangs make use of status and prestige to recruit and motivate.

I've observed some relatively downscale used car dealerships treating their customers like royalty, with remarkable sales results. Every human being, regardless of their station in society, enjoys the exhilaratingly pleasurable feelings of status and prestige, and will pay to get it.

Snap-On Tools does a remarkable job of exploiting the natural human desire for S&P with tools marketed directly to professional mechanics. Through the use of high quality, high service, and high price, Snap-On has created a decided cachet for their brand of mechanics tools. And that is exactly why professional mechanics pay several times more for a Snap-On wrench than a Stanley, Craftsman, or Kobalt wrench. There's nothing wrong with Stanley, Craftsman, or Kobalt, you understand. They're decent quality, and even exude some S&P in their own right. But Snap-On is at another level entirely when it comes to status and prestige, due mainly to their much higher price and the relationship between the salesperson and buyer. In the professional garage environment, where mechanics congregate and observe one another, being seen by your peers as the owner of a top-of-the-line, prestigious Snap-On tool is the ultimate.

Package for Gifting

Another instance where S&P plays a key role in pricing is in gift buying. When it comes to buying gifts, the consumer's tendency to seek a discounted price is quite often negated. In fact, gift buyers oftentimes seek to pay a high price, so as to convey to the recipient that they (the gift giver) is a person of stature and means, and that they care about the recipient. When it comes to gift buying and gift giving, paying a low price can be a disadvantage. Think about how a gift buyer might commit relationship suicide by giving a bargain-priced gift.

"Here's your anniversary gift, honey . . . diamond earrings! And you won't believe this . . . they were only thirty-five buckaroos from some guy on the street corner!"

Or on the professional level:

"You've all done a spectacular job all year long . . . and we appreciate your dedication and loyalty. Therefore, I have for each of you a fourteen-dollar gift certificate to Bennie's Belly Bombers, where you can dine out with the whole family."

I'm not poking fun at anyone with limited financial means. After all, it really is the thought that counts when it comes to gift giving. But it is this precise element — the thought — that most often compels the gift giver to spend a lot of money on a gift. The gift giver wants to elevate their own level of status and prestige, as well as conveying some degree of care, appreciation, or love for the recipient.

My recommendation is to consider creating a gift-package version of your product or service. I have such a package in the planning stages right now, and it may be on the market by the time you read this. I'm creating a gift pack consisting of the book you are now reading, my first marketing book *Creating Demand,* and a few other business goodies. If you know anyone who is responsible for the success of a product, service, or business, then you ought to buy this package for them. And I'll do you a favor. I'll price it high so the recipient will immediately know that you, the giver, are a powerful person of impeccable standing with exquisite taste and uncompromising standards.

Another way to exploit gift buying is with a slogan that conveys S&P. Hallmark's classic line "When you care enough to send the very best" is a wonderful example. So is Visa's line "People treat you differently when you show them a Visa platinum card."

Using a status and prestige slogan must be done with caution, however. Blatant declarations of status and prestige, reeking of pre-tentiousness or pomposity, oftentimes backfire. Instead, be subtle with your declarations and let the consumer assess your level of S&P for themselves.

Does Your Package Project S&P?

If you're attempting to project a higher level of status and prestige, your physical package is critically important. What the buyer sees affects their perception of your product's value.

Jewelers do an outstanding job with this. From the plush, elegant design of their physical store, to the display cases and velvet cloth upon which the jewelry is displayed, S&P is generously exuded. It doesn't end there. When you purchase a piece of jewelry, the jeweler places it in an expensive-looking gold embossed box, which in turn is placed inside an equally elegant bag.

Packaging — what the buyer sees — is equally important for services. If your service is high-priced, you'd better look the part. Plush offices in Class A office space, ornate stationery, lush vehicles.

Don't forget your appearance, or that of the executives or sales-people. Ever notice that the employees of jewelry stores are always impeccably dressed and groomed? Same with financial advisors and high-end real estate agents.

You may think you look great, but you probably don't. Your fif-teen-year-old hair style, worn suit, and frumpy shoes are giving you away. If status and prestige is part of your marketing effort, and personal selling comes into play, you may want to use the ser-vices of an image consultant to help with your appearance.

Conditions for S&P Success

You may still be doubtful that the Project Status and Prestige strat-egy will work for you, and you may be right. It works great for some, and not nearly as well for others.

The two conditions under which this strategy works best are:

1. **You market directly to the end user.** The end user will value, and pay handsomely for, status and prestige. But if you mar-ket to middlemen and not the end user, it will be much more difficult for you to use status and prestige as a means of rais-ing your prices.

    Let's say, for example, you manufacture and market indus-trial chemicals to boat manufacturers. To the boat manufac-turer, your customer, your chemicals are just plain old raw materials. To maximize their own profit they want to keep their costs as low as possible. They aren't interested in any status or prestige when buying raw materials. They are interested in exuding S&P themselves when they market to the end user, but that benefits them, not you. Think of it this way: Status and prestige is like frosting on the cake. The question is, who adds — and profits from — this frosting? Most likely, it's the party that markets to the end user that applies the status and prestige frosting and bumps up the price accordingly.

2. **Your product or service can be seen when in possession of the buyer.** It's a visual thing most often. Products like automobiles, clothing, furniture, houses, pens, wearable accessories, office space, and iPhones are obvious examples. For services, status and prestige must be visible in the marketing. This would be the exquisite brochures, impeccably dressed salespeople, plush offices, or lush vehicles I mentioned earlier.

   The less visible, or "on display" your product or service is when in possession of the buyer, the more difficult it is to use S&P to your advantage. If, for example, you market a pain relief ointment, its use will not be visible to anyone. The buyer might mention it to someone else if they're really pleased with its effectiveness, but such positive word-of-mouth happens for reasons other than to gain status and prestige.

If both these conditions are working in your favor, you are in excellent position to use status and prestige as a price levitator. If one of the two conditions is working for you, you may still be able to use this strategy, but the results will be less dramatic. If neither condition is working in your favor, this is probably not the right strategy for you.

Alert: Don't Sell the Exact Same Thing.

We determined that consumers will pay a premium for something that conveys status and prestige. Yet this "want to pay more" premise seemingly contradicts the vast amount of evidence that tells us people want to pay the lowest price possible, save money, get a deal. There really is no conflict here. People will pay a lot for S&P, yet they seek to pay the lowest available price for the same thing. You may be willing to pay $35,000 for a watch, but if you can get that exact same watch at another place down the street for $32,000, you'll buy from the place that gives you the better deal.

The key is *same thing.* You can charge a high price for something that projects status and prestige, but if it's the same thing that someone else is selling, price competition will come into play.

Chapter Five

Induce Confidence and Trust

You've determined it's time to get a new roof put on your house. You have two choices. You could hire Company A, which you have a great deal of confidence in, or you could save some money by hiring Company B, although you don't have as much confidence in B's ability to get the job done right. Which company would you choose?

In this instance, where getting quality work and a leak-proof roof is important, most people would choose the company they trusted the most. Even if doing so meant paying more.

In situations where there is a lot at stake, and when the buyer will be held accountable for their decision, they will most often choose to pay more in exchange for feeling confident that things will turn out right.

Absolute Confidence and Trust

FedEx relies heavily on this concept. Their classic slogan "Absolutely, positively overnight" said it all. With FedEx, your important package will get where it is supposed to, when it is supposed to, without fail. Do people willingly pay about 40 times more to send a letter overnight with FedEx than they do to send the letter via First Class Mail with the United States Postal Service? Absolutely, positively they do.

Price and C&T are Directly Related

One of the ways you can induce confidence and trust in the buyer is to charge a high price. As with status and prestige, confidence and trust are directly proportional to price. Also, as we did with status and prestige, we'll consider confidence and trust one entity, and refer to them collectively as C&T for short.

I personally stumbled upon the direct relationship between C&T and price way back in '90s during a consulting project. After an all-day meeting with the client, I finally settled into my hotel room and relaxed. I popped on the TV and just watched whatever came on. It happened to be an old episode of "Matlock." The Matlock character, played wonderfully by the late Andy Griffith, is a defense attorney that takes on seemingly impossible cases and, of course, wins all the time. One of the character's traits is that he charges a $100,000 fee to represent someone, an amount considered very high at the time (in fact, seems high to this day).

It was Matlock's high fee that suddenly became an issue in this particular episode. One of Matlock's colleagues asks him why he charges his clients so much. "So they pay attention to me and do what I say," he replied.

Eureka! I jumped out of bed, grabbed a pen and paper, and made sure that keeper didn't get away. I knew I'd just witnessed a life-altering piece of advice, albeit from a fictional character.

Up until this memorable day, I'd been charging a modest, middle-range consulting fee. Now I realized that if I wanted to induce a higher level of confidence and trust in my clients, resulting in them paying utmost attention and acting upon my recommendations, I'd need to raise my fee.

As soon as I raised my consulting fee — out of the modest range and into the expensive range — a miraculous thing happened. Prospects expressed a heightened desire to do business with me. And clients displayed a higher level of respect and consideration. I even had one client introduce me to his staff by saying "Rick is high-dollar so I want you to pay attention and do what he says."

Just as a higher price can contribute to a higher level of confidence and trust in the buyer, a lower price can result in lower C&T, which can negate a sale.

When three different vendors each submit a price quote on some project, which one do buyers tend to choose — the lowest, highest, or the one in the middle? Most often, it's the one in the middle. There is a tendency, correctly or not, to view the lowest price as suspect (unless the product or service in question is known to be exactly the same).

Price and C&T are mutually beneficial. A higher price helps bolster confidence and trust, and confidence and trust supports a higher price. But it's not that simple. A high price alone, without more solid substance backing it up, is not going to be effective. Most likely, you will need to utilize one or more of the following attributes to create substantial, enduring confidence and trust.

The Guarantee or Warranty

A guarantee or warranty strengthens confidence and trust, thereby adding to the support structure of a higher price. At least it's supposed to work that way. However, there are two problems with guarantees or warranties that sometimes negate their ability to benefit you or the buyer.

The first problem is *unclear cash-in*. For a guarantee or warranty to have enough muscle to support a higher price, it must be clear to the buyer how such a guarantee would be redeemed or cashed in. Unfortunately, all too many marketers tout their wonderful guarantee on one hand, and purposely hide any instructions as to how this guarantee could be redeemed on the other hand.

I bought a gallon of wall paint recently, and noticed the rather large words "lifetime guarantee" on the front of the can. Just what does this mean? First of all, whose lifetime are they referring to, the paint manufacturer's, mine, the wall I paint, what? Secondly, how would I cash in on it? Let's say 23 years after painting I notice some chipping or peeling. Do I then call the paint manufacturer (if I could still locate them after a typical series of buyouts, mergers, or relocations) and demand a refund? Will they require me to ship them portions of the wall or paint chips as proof of the problem? Perhaps they'd expect me to ship them the empty paint can or the sales receipt to prove it was their paint that broke down. Would all this be worth the hassle? As you can see, this type of "lifetime guarantee" does not carry much weight. And the buyer shouldn't be expected to pay extra for it.

To remedy this problem, and give your guarantee some real bite, make redeeming it simple and clear. Craftsman tool's lifetime guarantee is a great example of doing it right. If a Craftsman tool ever breaks, you simply take back and they replace it on the spot. No questions, no hassle. Back when Sears was the exclusive Craftsman dealer (it's now Lowes), I once took an old, damaged Craftsman screwdriver into Sears and the salesguy took one look at it, tossed it into a barrel, went to the shelf and handed me a new one. That's a great way to create loyal customers.

The second problem with guarantees or warranties is that they can suffer from pervasiveness. If every brand or seller offers the same guarantee, then the guarantee becomes a mere *hygiene factor* (its presence goes unnoticed, but its absence would be a noticeable negative). You may need to offer a guarantee or warranty just because it's expected, but that guarantee or warranty just keeps you competitive and isn't going to support a noticeable price differential.

Make The Guarantee or Warranty Work for You

Are you ready to offer the type of guarantee or warranty that will support a higher price and generate more business? If so, offer one that is (a) uncommon in your industry, and (b) clear and simple to redeem.

Addressing a trade association of professional painters a few years ago, I was relating the story of what happened when I had my house painted. I mentioned that it seemed odd, and somewhat disconcerting, that the owner of the painting company, who communicated with me several times to sell the job, never called afterward to ask if I was satisfied. When the job was done, they just disappeared. Turned out I was happy with the work, and was willing to give him a testimonial and even a referral, had he just called. But since he never contacted me after the job was done, I really began to question whether that painting company was worthy of referral. And when a neighbor asked who did the work, I mentioned the name of the company with reservation. "They were okay, but not great," I said.

At the seminar, one of the painters raised his hand and said "We feel lucky if we can get paid and get out of there before they complain." To which just about every painter in the room blurted out "Yeah, all they do is complain."

I asked them what would happen if one painting company operated differently than that. What would happen if that one painting company offered a satisfaction guarantee and called afterward to make sure the customer was happy. Perhaps they would even schedule a post-job visit to do any desired touch up.

"Would this painting company be successful?" I asked.

The room fell silent for a few seconds. I could see the wheels turning in their collective heads. Finally one of them said "They'd get all the business."

A few years ago I bought new carpeting from The Home Depot. About two or three days after it was installed, a Home Depot representative called to check on things and to find out if I was satisfied. I said the carpeting looked great, the installation was perfect, and I was very satisfied. But what if I weren't satisfied? What would they have done to make me happy? They would have come back and fixed the problem, that's what. Here's an important point: Whatever it cost them to return and fix is made up thousands of times over in positive word-of-mouth, referral, and repeat sales.

My mother just purchased a new central air conditioning system for her home in southwest Florida from Ellsworth's Heating & Cooling. Ellsworth's proactively acted upon their own satisfaction guarantee automatically, without my mother having to say anything. A few days after the installation, they sent an inspection team — different people than the installers — over to examine everything and make sure it was installed properly and working properly. And they were prepared to make any adjustments or fixes if necessary. This procedure really bolstered my mother's confidence and trust in Ellsworth's, and in her mind justified the price she paid.

But back to those get-the-money-and-run painters. I suggested they seriously consider offering a satisfaction guarantee and setting up procedures for return visits to ascertain and fix problems. I gave them three good reasons why doing so would be advantageous.

First, by contacting the customer after the job is finished to assure happiness, you're really injecting a high dose of confidence and trust. Enough to charge a higher price to begin with (by touting the hassle-free, satisfaction guarantee). If you're looking for a way to stop competing strictly on price, look no further.

Second, the satisfaction guarantee follow-up is a wonderful marketing technique. You'll generate incredible word-of-mouth (the best and cheapest form of advertising), plus get testimonials and referrals. You could use the return-visit guarantee to create a never-ending stream of new and repeat business.

Third, it's only a matter of time before some new painting company offers such a guarantee and runs all over you. I pointed out in Chapter Two that most innovation comes from outside the particular industry in question. Sooner or later someone is going to come along and disrupt how things are bought and sold in your industry, and they'll probably do it with a strong dose of confidence and trust. Why let someone from outside your industry innovate and cash in? Why not you? Why not right now?

Testimonial Proof

Testimonials from satisfied customers, which are proof of results, can be a powerful C&T inducer. Or, they can be totally benign. It really depends on how they're used.

If showing testimonials is not typically used in your industry — if your competitors aren't doing much of it — then you have a golden opportunity to use them successfully. You could collect simple one-or-two-sentence comments from customers and show them any number of ways: on your website, in your advertising, in brochures, in sales presentations.*

If you market business to business, industry-specific testimonials can be extremely effective. Business buyers tend to want what their colleagues or competitors have. When you flash testimonials from others your prospect knows or competes with, you're really stimulating the buyer's "got to have what they have" hormones. Before you have any testimonials to show, you may not be ready to raise your prices. But once you have a good number of testimonials behind you, you're well positioned for a price increase.

---

*You'll probably need to secure permission to use a person's or business's name. This is typically done by asking them to sign a release form granting you permission to use their name and/or likeness and what they said for marketing purposes.

Confidence and Trust is the Frosting

Television infomercials make liberal use of testimonials from satisfied users, but it's usually not to induce confidence and trust. That would be too big a stretch. Infomercials shoot a never-ending stream of testimonials at you just to gain some believability and credibility, a level below confidence and trust. Since the products advertised on infomercials tend to promise Herculean results, they've got to work very hard just to rise above normal scepticism.

Have you noticed while all those giddy satisfied customers gush about the fantastic results they've gotten with the super-duper miracle gobbinator, three tiny words — "Results Not Typical" — are superimposed on the screen? Let's see now, if positive results are not typical, then negative results must be typical. No wonder the darn products never work nearly as well as they show on TV.

I recommend a different marketing model than what you see utilized in many infomercials. I believe the quality of the actual product or service should be strong enough to get you over the believability and credibility hurdle. Then your testimonials become the cherry on top.

Expressed in Advertising

Depicting confidence and trust in your advertising, including the use of well-written slogans or point lines, can add effective sizzle. You can, in fact, get a double-barreled hit when you not only bolster confidence and trust in your product or service, but simultaneously cast doubt on your competitors.

State Farm seems to come up with a good number of ways to induce confidence and trust in their advertising. Sometimes they just come right out and say it. "Get yourself a State Farm agent or be left out in the cold," is a wonderful point line they've used. Sometimes they're a bit more subtle. One of my favorite State Farm television commercials shows what can happen when you have "cut-rate insurance." They show some poor sap who just smashed his car and can't get his insurance company on the phone, while Connie Francis is singing "Who's Sorry Now."

Fram oil filter's classic line "You can pay a little more now or a lot more later" implies that a less expensive oil filter will give you trouble. Plus, it justifies paying more for a Fram filter.

Maytag induces C&T by showing their repairman never having anything to do. FedEx has for years depicted business people who have chosen another shipping company, experienced a lost package, and ended up looking like idiots in front of their office peers.

A Weak Link Will Wreck Confidence and Trust

When you induce confidence and trust, build it and cultivate it over time, and use it to support a higher price, you cannot afford to have that delicate structure come crashing down. And a weak link in your operation will crash your C&T structure.

Let's look at one example where the marketer understands this, and thereby benefits greatly by utilizing confidence and trust, and another example where the marketer fails to understand this and thereby cannot use confidence and trust to any advantage.

FedEx and UPS (both are equally good examples) assure you they will deliver your package to the right address by the right time without fail. They back it up with mammoth, detailed logistical systems, precise package tracking, and fast, responsive customer service. They deliver (no pun intended) a heavy dose of C&T, and charge accordingly.

They also lose money on some shipments here and there, when the cost of delivering a particular package exceeds what they charged for that package. Examples would include delivery to an out-of-the-way address, or sending out a helicopter to rescue packages in a broken down truck, or sending another jet to an airport with a malfunctioning jet, or locating a package that did become temporarily lost. FedEx and UPS will absorb whatever costs are necessary to maintain their promise of on-time, worry-free delivery, in each and every case. In other words, they make sure there's no weak link in the system. For the system, and all the on-time, worry-free confidence and trust they've so painstakingly cultivated over the years, is supremely important. FedEx and UPS cannot afford delivery failures, because they cannot afford to lose the confidence and trust their customers pay alot for.

Then there are others that cannot seem to grasp this concept. They expect each division, each project, or each product or service, to produce equally high margins each and every time. If one division, project, product, or service is not delivering the margin they expect, they cut expenses in that area, without regard for building or maintaining confidence and trust.

The perfect example is most radio stations. Because the listening audience will be less late at night and on weekends, some stations cut their expenses during these times and air sub-par programming. Some stations have taken it to an extreme, where they have no live announcer, newscaster, or disc jockey on duty at all in the evenings, middays, or weekends. Nothing but a computer playing music and pre-recorded "voice tracks" of disc jockeys (made to sound live), or simply running a network show. If you listen for any length of time and never hear the station give the time, or hear a vague, general weather report without the current temp, you're probably listening to a computer, nothing more. An incredibly weak link, but one which many radio stations accept because it reduces expenses.

It also reduces confidence and trust. A couple years ago around 11pm I was driving in a bad wind and rain storm. I tuned into the local news/talk radio station for information, and heard nothing but a network show (originating in a distant city), with no mention whatsoever of the immediate weather situation. Arriving at my destination some twenty minutes later, I saw a local television station with live reports of the tornado that was swirling through the area, knocking trees down and flooding streets. Is it any wonder that local television stations, despite ever-growing competition from cable and satellite channels, still attract large audiences and charge ever-higher advertising rates? Meanwhile, radio stations struggle for listeners and advertisers. Which is earning your confidence and trust — a radio station that's asleep at the wheel or a television station that's on top of everything moment by moment?

Nickel n' Dimeing 'Em Will Wreck C&T

When you induce confidence and trust, and use that to command a higher-than-average price, you will be expected to "make it right" without charging extra. After all, that's what confidence and trust is all about. The buyer trusts you to make sure whatever they're buying is going to turn out or work exactly as it's supposed to. They have the confidence in you to do whatever it takes to assure their satisfaction. So, you would be wise to build a reasonable amount of follow-up or product adjustment into your modus operandi.

The practice of charging extra for every little thing is indicative of discounters, and it may work for them. But if you sell at a premium price, more is expected (as part of what they're paying for). The combination of premium pricing and charging for minor extras is deadly.

Alert: Induce by Earning.

This chapter is entitled Induce Confidence and Trust, meaning you create, build, and grow that state in the buyer's mind. However, confidence and trust is not a psychological facade. Someone who sells confidence and trust with no substance behind it is merely a con artist, not a legitimate marketer. Inducing genuine confidence and trust is based on superior quality and execution, unwavering over time. In other words, you earn it. Each and every day. Only when buyers know it's for real will they reward you by gladly paying a higher-than-average price.

Chapter Six

Rotate Standard

This strategy is all about creating a new, standard size or configuration of product or service, along with a new, higher price to go along with it. If you have a product or service that is purchased with some regularity, the Rotate Standard strategy may be something to consider.

Don't Just Toss and Hope

Your objective is for your new size or configuration to become the new standard, that is, the most preferred and most often purchased. And for your accompanying higher price to become standard also. Accomplishing that is not quite as simple as creating a new, larger or smaller size, tossing it into the marketplace, and hoping it flies. There are more sophisticated methods for increasing the odds of success.

The three best methods of rotating standard are The Soda Maneuver, The Combo Maneuver, and The Downshift Maneuver. Here's how they work:

The Soda Maneuver

The soft drink industry pioneered this method decades ago. Since just about all the soft drink brands tend to move in unison, we'll collectively refer to them as "the sodas" to maintain simplicity.

For many years, the 12-ounce bottle was the standard size in the soft drink industry. (At this early stage of our discussion, we'll focus on soft drink bottles and deal with cans later.) In fact, the 12-ounce bottle was so ubiquitous it was hard to find any other size. Then one day the sodas got the idea of offering their product in a larger 16-ounce bottle. So far so good.

Here's where it gets interesting. When they introduced the 16-ounce bottles, they priced them the same as the 12-ounce bottles, touting "four free ounces" in each bottle.

Let me ask you, if you saw 16-ounce bottles right next to 12-ounce bottles on the grocery store shelf — each priced the same — which would you buy? Of course, everyone chose the 16-ounce bottles. In no time, sales of the 16-ounce bottles skyrocketed and sales of the 12-ounce bottles plummeted.

Here's where it gets even more interesting. When sales of the 12-ounce size disintegrated, they pulled the 12-ouncers off the market. Since consumers were overwhelmingly choosing the 16-ounce size over the 12-ounce size, why bother keeping the undesirable 12-ouncers around?

Here's where it flies off the interesting scale and rings the payoff bell. With the 16-ounce bottles having supplanted the 12-ounce bottles as the new standard size, and the 12-ouncers gone, they stopped offering the "extra" four ounces for free and began charging for them. In other words, the price went up. They now sell more product for more money.*

Oops — They Did it Again

Have you seen 16-ounce bottles of soft drinks on the grocery shelves lately? No? Well perhaps you see stacks of 20-ounce bottles. In the mid-'90s the sodas rotated to 20-ounce bottles, which supplanted the 16-ouncers as the standard size.

— And Again

Perhaps you don't see 20-ounce bottles after all. No sooner did the 21st century roll around when the soft drink industry (as I said before, all the brands seem to move in unison, so it's impossible to credit any one brand as leading the change) executed The Soda Maneuver yet again. In some stores it's hard to find 20-ounce bottles whereas 24-ounce bottles are everywhere.

By the time you read this, perhaps the 24-ouncers will be gone and a different size will be the standard. (Remember, they've executed The Soda Maneuver several times over several decades. Coca-Cola and Pepsi-Cola originally started with a 6.5-ounce bottle as the standard size!)

---

*On an ounce-for-ounce basis, the price may be higher, lower, who knows. Because the price of soft drinks is constantly in flux, we can't use this measure in this discussion. Instead, we'll simply concern ourselves with the gross revenue The Soda Maneuver produces.

Also, the liter, as opposed to the ounce, is a popular measure used in the soft drink industry, but addressing that dimension here would complicate our discussion and not add to our understanding of the material.

Slow Motion Replay

The Soda Maneuver is actually a series of four distinct steps. They are:

- **Step One: Offer a larger size or otherwise greater configuration at the same price as your smaller, lesser configuration.** Draw attention to the fact that the buyer gets a "bonus" or "extra" amount for "free" with the greater configuration.

- **Step Two: Allow time to go by, as buyers exercise their right to choose.** Under normal conditions, they'll overwhelmingly choose the greater configuration because it's obviously the better deal.

- **Step Three: When sales of the lesser configuration have sufficiently dwindled, take it off the market.**

- **Step Four: Discontinue offering the bonus amount for free.** When the bonus amount is no longer free, you have effectively raised the price.

As I stated at the outset, with The Soda Maneuver you've created a new, larger preferred size, at a higher price point. And the consumer has helped you do it. It is the consumer, after all, who has overwhelmingly chosen to purchase the larger configuration. They're actually the ones who've made it the new standard, not you. The buyer has voluntarily raised the amount of product they purchase and amount of money they spend, and you are the beneficiary of that.

You Can Adapt the Strategy to Suit Your Circumstance

As I've described them, the four steps appear clear and well-defined. But in real-world application they are often blurred. Said another way, you don't have to follow the steps precisely to have an effective result. Feel free to adapt them to fit your particular situation.

For example, Step One of The Soda Maneuver states that you should offer a larger size or otherwise greater configuration at the same price as your lesser configuration. You may not be able to do this, however, if your greater configuration is a major jump up, like going from a 6-pack to a 12-pack. Six additional units — double the previous amount — may be too much to offer for free. In cases like this you could (a) adjust the price of the smaller configuration upward, and (b) price the newer, greater configuration at an amount that makes it obviously the better deal.

Step Three says you take the lesser configuration off the market once sales have sufficiently dropped off. However, many marketers prefer to keep their lesser configuration on the market instead of discontinuing it, even when sales have dwindled. In fact, even the sodas continue to produce their product in a variety of sizes to accommodate various retailer preferences. It's just that the larger configuration bottles have become the new standard, which prohibits most retailers from stocking all those other various sizes, given a limited amount of available shelf space.

Also, the speed at which you move through the four steps can vary from a few weeks to a year or more, depending on how frequently your product or service is purchased. Whatever speed you go however, keep this objective in mind: If you're going to discontinue the lesser configuration, wait until after the marketplace has had ample time to ignore it. You don't want to jolt the customer into realizing an option is being taken away. You take an option away only after the customer no longer cares about it.

Same Maneuver, Different Container

Continuing with the soft drink example . . .

What about cans (as opposed to bottles)? Same strategy, slightly different execution. With cans, size stays the same — 12 ounces — but the number of them in the package changes.

Remember when the 6-pack used to be the standard? Eventually the 6-pack was supplanted by the 12-pack, which has been the new standard for several years. However, soft drink manufacturers, along with beer manufacturers, are aggressively marketing 24-packs, which are on their way to becoming the new standard.

Applies to Many Different Industries

Because we're focusing on soft drinks to illustrate, and The Soda Maneuver gets its name from that industry, don't get the impression it's strictly for that industry. Quite the opposite. The Soda Maneuver works in just about any industry. Here are some examples:

- Two summers ago I purchased a can of insect repellent which had these big, bold words on the can: "Bonus size. 33 percent more. 8 ounces at the 6-ounce price." Looks like Step One of The Soda Maneuver to me. One year later I went to the same store to purchase another can. Sure enough, this time the only size cans available were the 8-ouncers, and they had no "bonus size" markings on them. The price was also higher than it was a year earlier. Steps Two through Four had been executed over the course of a year.

- Some amusement parks have shifted from the single-day pass to the two- or three-day pass as the standard. They still make the single-day pass available, but it's clearly the worst deal, and therefore chosen much less than the multi-day pass.

- Many fast-food restaurants have shifted from selling primarily single items to aggressively emphasizing their multi-item "value meals" or "combo deals." In the short run, this raises the average amount of each purchase. In the longer run, once the consumer is in the habit of buying these multi-item breakfasts, lunches, or dinners, the restaurant is in position to raise the price. (More on this later.)

- Gillette introduces new razors every few years, each one with more blades than the last. The new ones always cost more than the ones they replaced, too. Within a year or two of a new launch, the old ones are no longer on the market. If you observe closely, you see The Soda Maneuver executed perfectly every time.

- Do you patronize any of the big-box membership stores such as Sam's Club, Costco, or BJ's Wholesale? Practically everything in these places is sold in large configurations, but not necessarily bulk discounted. (More on this later, too.)

- I'll bet other examples come to your mind. Think of things you used to purchase in smaller quantities or configurations and now purchase in larger configurations. Things you used to spend less on that you now spend more on.

Consumers Just Keep on Consuming

Rotating from a smaller configuration standard to a larger configuration standard brings up this interesting issue: If buyers switch from purchasing the lesser configuration to the larger configuration (in terms of unit size, or number of items in the package), then they will probably purchase less often, right? They probably consume the same amount of product over the same span of time, regardless of what size is purchased, wouldn't you conclude?

Logical reasoning, but inaccurate. As it turns out, people do not consume the same amount over the same span of time. In fact, *consumption tends to expand to match that of what is available.* Like goldfish that will eat all the food available to them at any given time, humans tend to do the same.

Put a 12-ounce bottle of soda pop in the consumer's hand and he'll drink 12 ounces. Put a 16-ounce bottle in his hand and he'll drink 16 ounces. Twenty-ounce bottle, 20 ounces down the hatch. Yes, sometimes people will drink a portion and save the rest for later. But later is usually minutes or hours, not days. As it turns out, people are buying the greater configurations just as frequently as they used to buy the lesser configurations.

Here are a few more examples of this phenomenon:

• Retailers have discovered that if they provide larger carts, shoppers tend to fill those carts with more items. Personally, I've noticed it's hard to find small hand-held baskets at the Walmart and at the Costco near my house, yet those large push carts are abundant. Come to think about it, those large carts seem to be getting larger all the time. No matter what the size cart, shoppers tend to fill them to the brim, don't they?

- As mentioned earlier, membership warehouses, such as Costco and Sam's Club, base a great deal of their success on the fact that customers tend to prefer larger configurations. People even choose the larger configurations when there's no price advantage in doing so. Offered four rolls of toilet paper for $3.00 or sixteen rolls for $12.00, people will often choose the 16-roll packages.

- The more television channels or subscription services that are available, the more time people spend watching TV.

- Before cell phones, people didn't spend anywhere near the amount of time they do now on the phone. But you put a phone in someone's hand, provide them with unlimited everything, and they talk, talk, talk, text, text, text nonstop.

- Last spring I purchased 8 cubic yards of hardwood mulch and spread it all over my property. This spring I purchased 10 cubic yards of the stuff, and somehow this larger amount covered the same amount of land. Next year I'll probably get 12 cubic yards, and it'll probably disappear over the same amount of land. Why? Who knows why. It just does.

Of course, there is a point of diminishing returns, when consumption saturation occurs. If this were not the case, your typical consumer would be drinking an 84-ounce bottle of cola by day, putting away a 72-pack of beer by night, never taking their eyes off the television, and never putting down the cell phone. Except for teens with cell phones glued to their heads, most adult people find there is a practical limit as to what they will consume within a certain time frame. (We have a way to deal with that, which we'll get to later in this Chapter.)

The Combo Maneuver

Like The Soda Maneuver, The Combo Maneuver is a specific method of Rotating Standard. And like The Soda Maneuver, The Combo Maneuver is adaptable to just about any industry.

I'm sure you're familiar with fast food restaurants and their "combo meals" or "value meals." It's your basic package deal with three or four items bundled together and sold as a unit. The package price is less than what it costs if you buy each item separately, which is what coaxes buyers to choose it. Whenever a buyer purchases your combo, you have effectively sold more product and raised the average amount spent per purchase.

Here's the actual procedures:

- **Step One: Bundle three to five items together and offer it at a package price** (less than what all the component items would be if purchased separately). You may want to create a unique name for your combo to aid purchase of it. See Chapter Seven: Brand It, for details on this last point.

• **Step Two: Allow time to go by as more and more buyers choose the combo.** This assumes you're promoting it, by the way.

• **Step Three: While your combo is on its way to becoming the new standard, raise the price of the individual components in your combo.** Notice I did not say raise the price of the combo. Rather, raise the price of the individual items; what the buyer pays if they choose to buy individually.

This Step makes the combo an even better deal, which adds even more incentive to choose it.

• **Step Four: When your combo is firmly entrenched as the standard configuration, raise its price.** The likelihood that this price increase will result in lower sales of the combo is unlikely, since it's still the better deal compared to buying the individual component items (which underwent price increases earlier).

The Downshift Maneuver

When you've upsized your product or service with either The Soda Maneuver or The Combo Maneuver to the point of practical limit (which means it's as big as it's ever going to be), what next? You Rotate Standard in the opposite direction. In other words, you downshift to a smaller configuration.

The Downshift Maneuver is the exact opposite of The Soda Maneuver or The Combo Maneuver. Instead of introducing a bigger, greater configuration, you introduce a smaller, lesser configuration. Instead of introducing your lesser configuration at a low price initially, you introduce it at a higher price.

Why would the consumer prefer it over your greater configuration, especially when it's not discounted? Because he or she is getting tired of buying bulk, that's why. When your standard configuration has become very large over the years, the consumer may be ready for a drastic change of pace. Give 'em a break. Take 'em in the other direction for a while.

A few years ago, the colas introduced their product in the then new 8-ounce cans. Compared to the standard 12-ounce cans, these shorter, stubbier cans looked pretty strange at first. They also priced them at a premium to their standard 12-ouncers. When I witnessed a friend placing both a pack of 12-ounce cans and a pack of 8-ounce cans of Coca-Cola Classic in her shopping cart, I asked why she was buying the smaller cans when they cost more than the larger cans (I was thinking on an ounce-by-ounce basis in this instance). "Because sometimes I don't want to drink a big can," she replied. Makes sense to me.

Break Up the Combo

- At high-end restaurants like Ruth's Chris and Morton's, each item is sold separately. The result is that the customer spends a lot more in total than at other restaurants where a dinner includes several items.

- Replacement parts for machines, such as automobiles, airplanes, printing presses, computers, and most others, cost a lot more individually than if you bought a whole bunch of the parts already assembled. Building your own car from parts is a heck of a lot more costly than buying one already built.

• In the world of audio/video equipment, every few years the trend swings back-and-forth between all-in-one systems and individual components. And whenever there's a rotation in standard from all-in-one to individual or individual to all-in-one, the price increases. (At least initially when new stuff first hits the marketplace.)

• An exterminator company offers their multi-point service on an annual contract basis, or they offer a specific individual service as a one-time purchase. Every few years the buying trend shifts from the larger, packaged configuration to the individual item configuration and vice versa.

My point is not the obvious fact that various businesses offer individual parts or bundled packages. It's all about creating new standard configurations, that is, emphasizing a newer configuration (whether it be larger or smaller), and persuading the consumer to choose it over the older configuration. And every time you Rotate Standard, you raise the price.

It's All About the Price of the Stock

Many large, publicly-traded companies are well-classed players of the Rotate Standard strategy. For example, to get the price of their stock moving upward, the public company will often go on an acquisition binge. When you buy or merge with another company, you add the acquired company's revenue to yours, resulting in a relatively quick and dramatic rise in your (the acquiring company's) revenue. Do this two, three, or more times in a row over a few years and you have a wildly growing company with an exponentially rising stock price.

Then, when the stock price flatlines due to investor boredom, they do the opposite. They break the company apart, selling off divisions or spinning off subsidiaries into separately-traded public companies. The downsizing is usually viewed favorably by investors because it's a fresh alternative to years of upsizing. The price of the stock usually rises as a result.

Alert: The Consumer Remains in Control.

When Rotating Standard, in either forward or reverse, you are not "forcing" a greater or lesser configuration upon the buyer. Rather, the buyer remains in control at all times and can choose whichever configuration they like.

In this sense, it is the buyer that voluntarily raises the amount of money they spend whenever they choose your newer configuration.

Chapter Seven

Brand It

You say you can't raise your prices because you sell a commodity? You say your competitors sell an almost identical product or service, requiring you to compete based on price whether you like it or not? And you see no way out of this dilemma? The Brand It strategy may help.

The idea is this: You take an otherwise plain, mundane, austere product or service and you turn it into a special, stately, statuesque product or service. And the way you do that couldn't be simpler. You create a brand name, design a cool-looking logo, and attach it to the product or service. (As you know, there's more to it than that. But let's start simple and augment later.)

Immediate Respect

When you adorn an otherwise plain vanilla product or service with a brand name and distinctive logo, you make a presumptive statement. Before any other attribute is up for consideration, you are stating that the item in question is of a significantly different, significantly superior ilk than that of other comparable non-branded items, by virtue of its brand name and distinctive logo. A branded commodity commands a higher level of acceptance and respect than a non-branded commodity.

For the most part, this élite interpretation of a branded commodity lives strictly in the consumer's subconscious mind, and apparent only when observing what buying choices the consumer actually makes. They almost always choose familiar brands over unfamiliar brands or generics.

The buyer's affinity for branded products and services also surfaces in marketing surveys, it turns out. Marveling over the inexplicable success of branded bottled water, for example, a number of organizations have conducted every consumer research study imaginable and found the same result: Your average consumer believes branded bottled water is of superior quality to non-branded tap water. Even though, it turns out, many brands of bottled water are nothing more than tap water. Quite often in taste tests, consumers will swear that branded water tastes vastly better than tap water, when it turns out the one they've selected as their favorite is, in fact, ordinary tap water.

Where the Power Comes From

A branded commodity gets its élite, statuesque status from three sources. To give it the most attractive power possible, you'll want to utilize all three.

The first source of power is *presumptive quality,* which is the one we've already discussed. Simply by creating a good brand name and cool logo, and attaching that to the product or service, you've immediately distinguished yourself as an above-the-pack item. As simple and superficial as this may be, it is effective. Think bottled water. It's just plain old water with a good brand name and logo attached.

The second source of attractive power is the *attitude* your newly-branded item exudes. I've devoted Chapter Eight: Exude Attitude, to this, so we won't go into it here.

The third source of power is one we will discuss in detail right now. It's called *controlled comparison*.

The controlled comparison technique involves comparing your branded item to another non-branded item, pointing out the branded item's superiority. The real secret is this: Both items you're comparing — the branded and the non-branded — are products or services that *you* offer. Do not compare to what the competition offers. This is where so many marketers of commodities go wrong. They fall into the trap of comparing to the competition. Remember, you choose what game to play. When you compare to the competition, you're playing a game that leads you down the low price road. My suggestion would be to play a different game. Compare to yourself and you're headed down the higher price road.

Compare to Yourself, Not to the Competition

Let's discuss a concrete example of controlled comparison, where two competing marketers compare to themselves and not to each other.

The Home Depot sells two different grades of lumber. There's the ordinary, standard grade, and there's the higher, premium grade. The standard grade has no brand name at all; it's just plain old lumber, a commodity. But their superior grade has a brand name, "Premium

Cut." And each piece of Premium Cut lumber has a logoed sticker or burned-in logo attached to it (this is important!). Needless to say, Premium Cut lumber is priced higher than the standard, non-branded lumber at The Home Depot.

What about Home Depot's main competitor, Lowe's? They do the same thing. Their standard grade of lumber carries no brand name, but their higher grade is branded "Top Choice." And the Top Choice logo appears on every piece.

Home Depot's Premium Cut lumber commands a higher price because it's a better grade than their ordinary, non-branded lumber. Lowe's Top Choice commands a higher price because it's a better grade than their ordinary, non-branded lumber. Comparing standard to branded, the consumer can ascertain the difference and understand why the branded costs more.

Now if you compare Home Depot's Premium Cut to Lowe's Top Choice, what makes one more special than the other? Nothing. They're virtually the same. And that's just fine; insignificant, really. Both Home Depot and Lowe's are smart — they're not comparing their respective brands of lumber to one another — that would force them both into a price war and dilute their nice margins. The Home Depot and Lowe's are fierce competitors for sure, but they're also "brothers under the sun" that know when to and when not to cross swords.

What if your main competitor starts comparing their branded commodity to your branded commodity in some ad campaign or the like? Rejoice — your competitor is an idiot. Price-warring commodities, branded or not, is a losing strategy. Doing so is not sustainable.

What about a company like HP (Hewlett Packard) that uses price as a comparison point relative to other brands of computer? Contrary to some opinion, I don't believe the personal computer is a commodity at all. When you buy an HP-branded computer, you gain a high level of confidence. Your new HP is a quality machine, and HP stands behind it with pretty good service and support. Those logical benefits alone make it a rarity, not a commodity, I would argue.

Inherent Quality

As I've stated several times throughout this book, when you price something above average, you have to justify that higher price with above average quality. I reiterate this point again, so you don't think I'm suggesting that a brand name alone, without any inherent quality boost, will do the trick.

However, there appears to be some rare exceptions to this. Bottled water may be one. Vodka may be another. According to industry insiders, some brands of premium or even ultra-premium vodka are no better quality than the average brand. In fact, some brands of low-grade and premium-grade vodkas are reported to be the exact same stuff just put into different bottles. Therefore it would appear that real, superior quality may not be necessary to command a high price in some instances, at a particular point in time. But why take that risk? Why not strengthen your new brand's attractiveness with real, discernible quality and reduce the chances of failure?

The winning formula is: Build higher-than-average quality into your product or service, make sure it's visible to the buyer, create a brand name and great looking logo, price it above average, and market to people who want to pay for the best. If you do it right, your added expense for the higher quality is returned many times over by the higher price. In other words, you can take advantage of the quality price/cost multiple. For every dollar you spend on improving the quality, you can add many more dollars to the price.

Love him or hate him as President of the United States, we have to give Donald Trump credit for expertly executing the Brand It strategy in his previous job as a real estate mogul. In that real estate role, he spent what was necessary to create top-of-the-line, tangible quality in his buildings. Then he attached the Trump name to it. Both the quality and the brand name embellished each other, with increasing magnitude over time. The quality and opulence gives the Trump brand name a high level of cachet and prestige. And the Trump name in turn anoints each property with that cachet and prestige. All this allows Trump properties to charge ultra high prices — and keeps demand high for just about anything sporting the Trump brand name.*

Branding the Ultimate Commodity

I mentioned bottled water earlier, and you must have known I couldn't let that one go without further comment.

Water is the ultimate commodity. After all, 70-percent of the Earth's surface is plain old water. Yeah, a lot of it is salt water. That can be converted to fresh, but why bother? There's so many lakes, streams, rivers, and springs that fresh water is readily available in just about every developed part of the world.

Much of it is free. Go to any restaurant, sit down and ask for a

---

*Two occurrences mitigated the Trump image somewhat. First, he licensed the name to other property owners, and some of them allegedly didn't keep up the same level of quality. Secondly, as POTUS his image became very polarized, with those in the "hate him" camp shunning his real estate properties.

glass of water. They'll set it down right smack dab in front of you, no charge. There are drinking fountains everywhere that shoot water right into your mouth, no charge. Water rains down upon us out of the sky. I don't know about you, but I can't ever recall getting a rain bill in the mail. Nor can I think of any other product so prevalent it falls right out of the sky.

Water is everywhere and it's free. (Or close to free. Unless you water your lawn 24/7, your home water bill can't be much.)

Yet bottlers (we can't call them "manufacturers" because there's nothing to manufacture) put it into half-liter bottles, slap a brand name on it, and sell it for 1,000 times what it costs for someone to get the same amount of water right out of their kitchen sink. And people buy it.

They buy tons of it, turns out. Bottled water is a thriving, multi-billion-dollar-a-year industry, with nice profit margins to boot. In fact, bottled water is so lucrative the two biggest soft drink manufacturers got into it in a big way several years ago. Coca-Cola owns the Dasani brand of water, Pepsi-Cola owns the Aquafina brand. And the number one seller of bottled water in the world turns out to be Nestlé, which markets not only the Nestlé and Perrier brands, but a variety of regional brands including Poland Springs, Deer Park, Arrowhead, Zephyrhills, etc. There are also a slew of smaller bottled water marketers doing quite well.

The Author's Branding Venture

I've long been fascinated by the bottled water craze. I confess that not only am I a buyer of bottled water, but I'm an inadvertent collector of obscure brands (seems I just can't throw out those empty bottles). If water is the ultimate commodity, then branding it is the ultimate branding experience.

I considered creating my own brand of bottled water, but the problem is I'm too far behind the curve on that. The proverbial "ground floor" is way too many floors below the playing field these days.

So I thought of two other innovative ways to get in the game ahead of the curve.

Idea one is to design and market a filter-like device that the consumer attaches to the end of their kitchen faucet. But unlike water filters that have been on the market for several years, my device doesn't do any filtering. It simply adds a brand name to the water that flows through it. Ordinary tap water goes in, branded water comes out (and into refillable, branded bottles that come with the device). This could be priced two different ways. Under one pricing option, the consumer pays one time when they buy the device and a couple dozen empty logoed bottles. It could be premium priced, since this system provides them with a lifetime supply of branded water for a one-time payment. Another pricing option is that the device is sold at cost, but the buyer pays premium prices for replacement logoed bottles, like the old razor/blade arrangement where most of the profit comes from replacement blades, not razors.

Idea two is even more revolutionary. Besides water, what is another major commodity that is (a) readily available everywhere for free, and (b) people consume every day? Air, of course. We are all constantly breathing air (technically the oxygen in the air). So the idea is to market a brand of bottled air.

You think I'm kidding. Yet I will tell you that I have indeed acted upon this particular idea, and with pretty good success. For several years now I have been marketing my own brand of bottled fresh mountain air. Check out my web site at RickOtt.com for more information.

As for idea one — the Incredible Miracle Water Brander — feel free to take that one and run with it. (If you're successful, I expect a cut. If you're unsuccessful, I expect you to forget where that idea ever came from.)

Others are Doing It

If it's possible to brand the ultimate commodity — water — and price it at 1,000 times more than cheap and plentiful tap water, and generate several billion in revenue, with fat margins, why can't you brand your commodity and do the same? Here's how some other marketers are doing it:

- Intel makes microprocessors, the "brains" inside computers. Unless you're a computer technician, and most people who buy and use computers are not, you'd never see the microprocessor nor would you even know what company made the thing. That was the problem Intel faced years ago. Their microprocessors could become a mere commodity if something wasn't done to prevent that.

    What did Intel do? First, they created brand names for their microprocessors. There was the Pentium, then the Xeon. Then the Core series. Certainly they'll have newer brand names as time goes on. Second, they arranged for their logo to appear on the boxes and even on the outside of the computers themselves. Third, they embarked on an "Intel Inside" ad campaign that brought all this to the forefront. The result? Intel's microprocessors have avoided the commodity quagmire, enabling Intel to maintain relatively high prices for their microprocessors.

- Chiquita brands their bananas. You've seen the stickers right on the bananas, haven't you? Most bananas are a commodity; one's as good as the next. Then there's Chiquita brand bananas. Better than average quality at a higher than average price.

- A plain polo shirt, with no logo on the front, costs around $12.00 at today's prices. But a similar shirt with LaCoste's alligator or Ralph Lauren's Polo player on it costs many times more than that. And the logoed ones sell really well.

- Put generic vegetables into a logoed bag like Dole does, and suddenly you've got your own brand of salad.

- Pharmacia & Upjohn market a hair-growing tonic called Rogain. It's the branded equivalent of the generic Minoxidil. Both Rogain and Minoxidil are available over-the-counter, usually sitting side-by-side on the shelf. One costs much more than the other, and it's that one that out-sells the other.

Speaking of that, do you remember generics? Those white-packaged, non-branded, non-logoed, low-priced versions of toilet paper, cigarettes, laundry detergent, breakfast cereal, etc? Whatever happened to generics? People didn't buy them, that's what happened. Consumers want brands, man, brands!

Anyone Can Brand

You don't have to be a manufacturer to create a brand. You can produce nothing and still create your own brand(s).

Grocery stores have been doing it for decades. They create their own house brand, then contract out the production. The Home Depot owns the Hampton Bay brand of ceiling fans and lighting fixtures. Home Depot buys the products from a variety of manufacturers, each of which simply sticks the Hampton Bay name on them.

You could, as many retailers tend to do, position your private label brand as a lower-cost alternative to comparable brands. But there is another way. Why not position your brand as a premium product or service? Most likely you'll have to communicate and demonstrate your brand's superior inherent quality. Plus you'll want to buttress your brand's higher price by using any one or more of the other strategies in this book.

A Brand Within a Brand

You can nest one brand within another brand, a configuration that tends to strengthen both brands simultaneously.

- When Verizon got into the cable television business, they branded their service Fios. In response, Comcast branded their service Xfinity. Now the sub-brands Fios and Xfinity can compete head-to-head on one level, as can their respective global brands Verizon and Comcast on a higher level.

- I mentioned Intel earlier. Intel, the name of the company, is a global brand. Core i5 and Core i7 are sub-brands.

- Walmart is a global brand. Their Great Value brand of food items is a sub-brand.

• Apple is the global brand; iMac and iPhone are sub-brands.

• The Vanguard Group is a global brand. Their 500 Index Fund, STAR Fund, and Wellington Fund are sub-brands.

A Brand Within a Brand Within a Brand

I see no disadvantage to creating numerous brands, and nesting each one within another. Note however that this is not the same thing as line extension. With line extension, you keep attaching the same brand name to more and more different products, a bad idea most of the time. But when you nest one brand within another, you create new brands for new products. Each product or service gets its own brand name (although the senior brand name can still appear).

• Ford Motor Company is a global brand. Lincoln is a sub-brand of Ford, and Navigator is a sub-brand of Lincoln.

• Anheuser-Busch is the global brand. Budweiser is a sub-brand of Anheuser-Busch, and Bud Light is a sub-brand of Budweiser.

• Proctor & Gamble is a global brand, Gillette is a sub-brand, and Fusion Razor is a sub-sub-brand.

Branding Makes it Easier to Describe, Easier to Sell

Why do you think they name hurricanes? Because doing so greatly aids communication. It's much easier and more precise to refer to Hurricane Katrina than it is to say "that hurricane that hit New

Orleans back in oh-five."

McDonald's has a bundle of food items especially for children which they've branded the Happy Meal. What if, instead of Happy Meal, they had no brand name for it? How would someone order it?

"I'd like that colorful box . . . and put some chicken nuggets in there, along with some fries and a kid's toy. And give me a small drink too," they might say. Or would it be easier to just say "I'd like a Happy Meal?" When you brand something, you make it easier for the customer to buy, and easier for you to sell.

This is especially true if you're trying to sell a variety of items bundled together, as in the Happy Meal example. And especially if your bundle contains some intangible services.

Make it Proprietary

When you brand a product or service, you've instantly created a *proprietary* product or service. It's all yours (assuming no one else has already trademarked the name in the same category or class). The marketplace tends to value a proprietary item higher than a generic or commonly available item.

If you market a service, why not make it a proprietary service? Or better yet, a proprietary *system*. When you systematize your service and adorn it with a brand name that is exclusively yours, you are in the best possible position to raise your price and simultaneously attract more business. In addition, your proprietary system takes on an air of tangibility, another attractive quality. Furthermore, a tangible, proprietary system is very conducive to media marketing. It gives you something to focus on; something to promote and create excitement about in your advertising.

Brand the Intangible

Intangible products and services can be branded, trademarked, and marketed as proprietary. Here are some examples:

- Six Sigma is a multi-stage management process designed to improve quality, which a number of large companies use. (It's actually owned by Motorola Solutions.)

- Tae Bo is a bunch of workout moves. Without the brand name it wouldn't be marketable for profit (but it might still be used). With the brand name, it becomes a proprietary entity that is marketable and profitable.

- "Electromagnetic radiation" is a generic term and therefore unmarketable for profit. Radio, the transmission of intelligence through electromagnetic radiation, is also a generic term. But Bluetooth is a trademarked brand name, based on proprietary technology, that is marketable for profit.

Brand Sentiment

If you want to promulgate adoption or opposition to a particular way of thinking or acting, create a one- or two-word name for it. Adoptive behavior or shunning behavior will spread much more rapidly. (A brand needn't be limited to an owned, trademarkable word. It can be a term you coin and toss around as a communication tool.)

Consider these terms: "Conservative," "liberal," "extremist," "due diligence," "big brother," "serial acquirer," "hero." People hear the term and understand the thinking it represents. They also tend to develop "for it" or "against it" sentiment.

- In the early 2000s, a number of large public companies imploded under the mismanagement of high-ranking officers who cooked the books. To correct this type of behavior, and to promote proper, above-board behavior, the term "corporate governance" surfaced. In rapid order, companies fell into line with much stricter corporate governance policies so as to conform to the new way of thinking.

- An attorney arguing a case may use a strong term that positively brands his or her client, and another strong term that negatively brands the opposition. Politicians tend to do likewise. For example, a politician may point the finger at "activist judges," as a way of arguing for stricter sentencing guidelines. A brand name is a handle that allows people to grab it, adopt it (or oppose it), and verbalize it to others in a way that spreads like sentiment.

- No one was diagnosed with "attention deficit disorder" until someone coined the term. Now every other kid — and a growing number of adults — are diagnosed with "ADD" or "ADHD" and prescribed some sort of treatment. Evidently you can create a market for your products and services by coining a new term to negatively brand the lack of it. I'm not a proponent of doing this, I merely make the observation to show how powerful branding can be.

Brand Yourself

You can turn yourself into a brand. John Deere, Jenny Craig, Martha Stewart, Jim Beam, Estée Lauder, Orville Redenbacher, Ralph Lauren, Charles Schwab, to name but a few, are "human brands." They started out as people and eventually became the brand name of a product, service, or entire company. (Some of them may, in fact, still be living, breathing people as well. But you don't even have to be a real living, breathing person to become a human brand. Betty Crocker, James Bond, Ann Taylor, and Fred Flintstone are human brands, although as you know, they never existed as real people.)

To become a human brand, attach both your first and last name to a product or service. You could even license your name to someone else (assuming someone would pay for it), Like John Elway did for the John Elway Home Collection brand of furniture (made by Bassett).

Can you use just one of your names — either first or last — as your brand name? You can, but that usually works best for naming an entire company, not a specific product. Ford Motor Company, Wendy's, Stanley Black & Decker, and the Smith and Jones law firm are company names, using last names only. To create a specific human branded product, it's best to use both your first and last name.

One final point about human brands: you need to define your human brand. It must mean something, stand for something. The consumer needs something to grab onto; something to recognize, believe in, and develop an affinity for. If you have a strong, attractive personality trait as a person, you could transfer that trait to your product, service, or business. If not, create a trait and personify your items accordingly.

Alert: Use Branding Carefully.

Using branding to guide public opinion, while done every day in advertising, law, and politics, may lead you into rough territory bordering on the manipulative or unethical. While it is my intention to discuss various applications of branding, it is not my intention to suggest you stray from its above-board application. (This is akin to the martial arts instructor warning his students not to go around hitting people just because they know how.)

Chapter Eight

Exude Attitude

Attitude sells. It can sell at a high price, in fact. Let's determine why that is, and see if you can sell attitude at a premium.

Humans Want Their Emotions Stimulated

People naturally want to feel certain emotions. Perhaps we want to feel we are loved and appreciated. Or perhaps we want to feel strong and tough. Or vulnerable and pitiful. Or funny and wacky. Or smart and resourceful. Or talented and creative. Or admired and respected. Or nonconformist and rebellious. You name it, people want to feel it.

How do we create these desired emotions in our brains? Usually through the aid of some emotional stimulators, which could be another person, or in the case we're concerned with, certain products, services, and companies.

Let's say, for example, you're a competitive person who relishes the feeling of winning. You see yourself as belonging to an élite group of talented performers who succeed despite tough odds and you want others to view you this same way. More than likely, when it comes to sportswear, your brand of choice will be Nike. Other brands may deliver the same high quality as Nike, but no other brand delivers the same élitist, winning attitude. (Which didn't happen by accident. Nike has deliberately and unwaveringly cultivated that image over several decades.)

Let's say I think of myself as an artist; a discriminating man of style and creativity who stands apart from the crowd. What brand of computer would you most likely find in my office — Dell, Hewlett-Packard, Lenovo, or Apple? All fine brands, but only the Apple exudes that artsy, nonconformist attitude I identify with. In other words, I feel a heightened level of creativity and artistry when I purchase and use Apple products.

It's the Association that Counts

Okay, we humans want to experience emotional feelings. That's because when our emotions are flowing (even negative emotions under certain conditions), our brain interprets that as a psychologically pleasing experience.

Most of the time our emotions lie dormant, anxiously awaiting to be stimulated. Like a stick of dynamite waiting to be lit. Along comes a particular brand that is exuding an attitude that appeals to us. So we purchase that product or service, because by *associating* with it our desired emotions are activated.

How does all this relate to elevated pricing? One could certainly buy some other brand of quality sports gear for less than what Nike-branded items cost. But with Nike, you get the élitist, winner attitude, which by association, makes you feel like an élitist winner. You gladly pay a premium for Nike products because it activates a special emotional feeling you enjoy. Certainly there are other ways to stimulate your élitist winner feelings, but buying Nike is just so easy.

Let me draw out the three important points here.

1. Your company or business needs to exude an attitude. Make your brand name an emotion detonator. (Assuming you choose to implement this Exude Attitude strategy.)

2. The buyer then gets his or her desired emotions stimulated by associating with your brand. In other words, they're attracted to it and have a strong propensity to buy it.

3. People will pay a premium for the privilege of getting their desired emotions stimulated. Especially when only one particular brand does the trick.

It's a Subconscious Function

I've stated that people innately want to feel certain emotions, and that they will associate with specific brands to stimulate those desired emotions. What I didn't say, until now, is that all of this happens subconsciously.

Consumers seldom consciously choose certain brands based on their ability to stimulate emotions. They don't logically reason this out. In fact, they're probably not even aware of it.

All you have to do is ask someone why they prefer Nike, Apple, Harley-Davidson, Coor's Light, Calvin Klein, Axe body spray, or any other attitude-exuding brand. Are they likely to say "I buy Nike because it stimulates my élitist winner emotions"? Doubt it. If they're able to articulate any reason whatsoever, which alone isn't easy, it's most likely going to be something based on superficial logic like "I drink Coor's Light because it goes down easy."

It Gets Better

There's more. Not only does the consumer want certain emotions stimulated in their own brain, and will pay well for that, but they also want certain emotions stimulated in other peoples' brains. And they'll pay even more for that.

Take the typical male that values the feelings of toughness, independence, and virility. What type of product would best stimulate these emotions — a bag of grass seed, a tunafish sandwich, or a motorcycle? And what brand of motorcycle best represents toughness, independence, and virility — Honda, Suzuki, Yamaha, or Harley-Davidson? So, our guy buys himself a Harley, even though he could have gotten another quality brand for less.

Simply owning the Harley — even if it just sat idle in his garage — would probably stimulate the guy's desired emotions, because of the association. He owns it, after all. It's his. And it exudes strength, toughness, and virility — that rubs off on him — just sitting in the garage.

But associating with the product in private may not be enough. Our macho man instinctively knows that his emotions can be stimulated far more when he displays or transmits. In fact, the intensity and sustainability of his emotions are heightened exponentially as more and more people become aware of his Harley. So he rides it in public whenever possible and tells as many people as he can that he owns a Harley.

If Jane buys a Nike pair of sneakers or Nike baseball cap or Nike sports bag or anything else with that famous checkmark logo, her association with the Nike brand stimulates the élitist, winner feeling she subconsciously values. But she can get an even stronger rush of that same élitist, winner feeling if she induces it in your brain as well. Not to make you feel like an élitist winner, mind you, but so you view her that way. So Jane wears or uses the Nike product in public, making sure you, along with everyone and anyone else, see her with it. Remember, Jane's self-image is that of a talented competitor who wins tough challenges. And she wants you to view her that way too. That's very important to her, and worth spending some serious money on.

If I buy an Apple iPhone, I want people to see me with it. I want them to view me as a cutting-edge, artsy, classy guy, and publicly displaying my association with the iPhone induces that emotional feeling in me. (This, by the way, is another great marketing move on Apple's part. They've turned an electronic product into a fashion statement. And Exuding Attitude is primarily how they do it.)

Again, let me remind you it's the emotional, subconscious part of the mind directing a person's behavior to prefer and buy something that exudes an attitude. But — and this is very important — the logical, conscious part of the mind needs to be satisfied also. Exuding Attitude can work wonders, but you will also need to provide the buyer with logical reasons or benefits for him or her to consciously consider and discuss. Attitude alone, without some solid, underlying logic, may not work. The iPhone, for example, has a superior, easy-to-use interface that consumers logically like.

It's a Company Thing

You may have noticed that the examples I've sited have been *com-*

panies exuding an attitude, not necessarily individual products or services exuding an attitude. In its most potent form, the Exude Attitude strategy is really a holistic, company-wide thing.

For this strategy to be most effective, it requires several years of accumulated attitude exposure to permeate the marketplace. And the more years that go by, assuming the same attitude is exuded all along, the stronger the effect. This is one of those things that is simple but not easy to execute. The difficulty is maintaining one consistent company attitude over time. When leaders and managers come and go, there's a tendency for attitudes to change. From an operational standpoint, a whole new attitude or culture may be a good thing if a failing company needs to be turned around. But from a marketing standpoint, it can be a bad thing if new managers fail to recognize the importance of maintaining the same strong, consistent attitude in the marketplace.

An Extension of the Charismatic Leader

When we look at the most successful companies that have implemented this Exude Attitude strategy, we see an interesting similarity. The company's attitude is really an extension of the charismatic leader's personality. Take Apple. Ever since it was founded, the company exuded its artsy, edgy, nonconformist attitude. Which was an exact extension of the late co-founder Steve Jobs' personality.

Nike's élite winner attitude is an extension of founder Philip Knight's personality. Southwest Airlines's happy-go-lucky attitude is a direct reflection of its founder's personality, Herb Kelleher. Tesla's elegant maverick attitude is an exact reflection of Elon Musk's personality. Fox Broadcasting, including their cable channels and over-the-air network, exudes a brash, irreverent attitude, which some have described as the personality of News Corporation (Fox's owner) founder and CEO Rupert Murdock.

As long as the charismatic leader remains at the helm, the prevailing attitude is likely to continue permeating and percolating. But what happens when the charismatic leader leaves? When Steve Jobs left Apple for several years in the mid-1980s and early '90s, Apple's attitude seemed to wain. Coincidently, Apple became somewhat directionless during this period and began floundering on several levels. When Steve returned in 1997, the artsy, nonconformist attitude returned with him, and Apple regained its strength. Since Steve's death in 2011, current Apple management seems to be smartly maintaining the attitude.

In the early 2000s, Nike founder Phil Knight relinquished his CEO position, as did Southwest Airlines founder Herb Kelleher. It will be interesting to see if their respective company attitudes remain healthy or if they slowly disappear under the new leadership.

Attitudes tend to be highly contagious. A charismatic leader's personality, including a strong, attractive attitude, will permeate the company. From there the attitude naturally permeates the marketplace. Enhance it with good, sustained marketing and you can create an irresistible attraction that translates directly into higher prices and more business.

Assuming a company is successful, ideally there would be no attitude change even though personnel change. An example would be Harley-Davidson. Senior management turns over, yet their tough, independent, virile attitude remains intact.

Individual Products and Services

Individual products and services, separate from their parent company, can exude an attitude also. But without a strong, supporting attitude on the part of the parent company, the individual product or service may have a tougher time exuding on its own, and is likely to be less potent in the marketplace.

Devoid of a strong attitude emanating from the parent company, a product's or service's attitude must come from some other source, and probably a weaker source. Usually the attitude source, if not from the parent company, is the relatively superficial ad campaign in effect at the moment. And ad campaigns, like ad agencies themselves, tend to change with great rapidity. Whatever the attitude-of-the-moment is, it doesn't seem to grow roots; it doesn't withstand the winds of marketplace volatility or internal company gyration. Therefore, individual product or service attitude is usually much less effective than company attitude.

However, there are exceptions.

Your average, generic teddy bear exudes no attitude. It's just a stuffed brown fur-like sack with two emotionless button eyes. For the generic teddy bear to have any personality traits, the owner would have to provide that with their imagination. But the Vermont Teddy Bear Company markets teddy bears that exude a whole lot of attitude. A wide range of different attitudes, in fact. There's the Stars and Stripes Bear that exudes a patriotic attitude (he's even got an American flag tattoo on his arm). There's the Feel Better Bear who's wearing a robe and is blowing his/her nose in a tissue. There's the Bahama Mama bear in sunglasses and swim suit. There are many others, each exuding a different attitude, separate from any company-wide attitude.

Coor's Light beer has exuded a raucous, party-party attitude in recent years, which is separate from the Molson Coor's company. Miller Lite seems to exude a somewhat quirky, screwball attitude, which is not necessarily the attitude of parent SABMiller. And Corona's relaxed, apart-from-the-crowd attitude may not necessarily be like the parent company at all. Like individual teddy bears and individual beer brands, any individual product or service can exude an attitude on its own. It can work. It just takes more unrelenting, forceful advertising to keep the attitude alive than if the attitude in question were exuded by the parent company.

Positive or Negative

The attitude you exude can be positive or negative.

Shoe Carnival exudes a fun, exciting attitude. Quicksilver (marketers of surf and skateboard apparel) exudes an energetic, confident attitude. Tesla exudes an elegant maverick attitude. We'll classify these as positive attitudes, since they usually are.

The Mondrian Hotel in Los Angeles, the Delano Hotel in Miami, the Royalton in New York, and a select few other non-chain hotels exude a heavy dose of an edgy, snobbish attitude (even to the point of being deliberately rude and disrespectful to guests). Some denim jean marketers sell "distressed" or "damaged" jeans with cuts, holes, and other abrasions, which exude a rebellious, don't-give-a-damn attitude. We'll classify these as negative attitudes, which is contextually how they're being used.

Whether it's positive or negative doesn't seem to matter. What does matter is that a clearly evident, unabashedly exuded attitude sells at a premium price. (If it seems odd to you that negative attitudes could be considered desirous, let me point out that those hotels I sited stay booked at around $250-$500 a night, and those worn-out jeans go for around $150-$200 a pair.)

Works on Any Scale

I tend to use major, national or international brands when I site examples, since you're most likely to be familiar with brands of this size. But you can exude an attitude on a much smaller scale with great results.

Restaurants and night clubs tend to be very good at Exuding Attitude, which attract like-minded patrons from the local marketplace.

Sports teams Exude Attitude, as do some athletes. In fact, athletes that exude just a little attitude now and then tend to enhance their celebrity status and elevate their market value for endorsements.

Alert: You Must be Comfortable
with Your Chosen Attitude.

You can exude just about any attitude you like, positive or negative. But you, or the top person in your company, must be comfortable with the attitude you exude or it's not likely to work. When the top person isn't comfortable with a particular attitude, that attitude tends to disappear.

Alert: Expect Heightened Polarization.

When you exude attitude, not only do you attract certain like-minded consumers, but you simultaneously repel certain other unlike-minded consumers. While it is quite normal to simultaneously attract and repel even when you don't exude an attitude, you will most likely experience a heightened degree of fervent supporters and fervent detractors when you do exude an attitude. Be aware, detractors come with the territory when you exude attitude. If you're not prepared for this, or if you can't stand an anti-your-company sentiment floating around, this strategy may not be for you.

Chapter Nine

Create a Premium Line or Economy Line

Perhaps, truth be told, the quality of your product or service really isn't all that high. Or perhaps, truth be told, you're already pushing the price limits of what the market will bear, and any further increase just won't fly. Perhaps, truth be told, your target market isn't going to increase their spending on what you sell no matter what you do.

Perhaps it's time to create a whole new line of product. Or even a whole new business. Your new line or business, whether it be a grade up or a grade down, can result in higher prices and more business.

Price Lining

The classic example of a company that pioneered the concept of having different product lines at different price points was General Motors in the 1920s. They discovered that the typical buyer of a Chevrolet could only afford to pay but so much. GM wasn't able to raise the price of a Chevrolet very much without pricing themselves out of that market. Upon acquiring Cadillac, GM priced it considerably higher than the Chevrolet, using it to target a different, wealthier segment of the marketplace. GM also had Buick and Oldsmobile operating in between the low and high ends. As history shows, it was this multiple-line strategy that allowed GM to overtake Ford as the nation's largest automobile manufacturer.

Speaking of Ford, they created the premium Lincoln line after they saw how well Cadillac was working. Other car manufacturers have done likewise. Honda has the Acura, Toyota has the Lexus, and Nissan the Infinity. It just makes so much sense to have both high- and low-end lines that doing so is now routine for automobile manufacturers.

A Whole New Premium Line

Dell was founded on the principle of selling computers at the lowest possible price. Over the years, Dell has become uniquely adept at developing production and marketing efficiencies, and at continuing to drive computer prices lower. Their low-price formula works very well for them.

Yet they were vastly under serving another, large segment of the marketplace: consumers who are willing to pay more to get more. So Dell created an entirely new line of premium-priced computers, complete with its own brand name, XPS. The XPS line includes high-quality machines with all kinds of whistles and bells, along with deluxe sales and support services. If you want to pay $400 for a computer, Dell has one for you. If you want to pay $4,000 for a computer, with their XPS line, Dell now has one for you, too.

Another Whole New Premium Line

McDonald's was founded upon the high volume/low price concept as well, and they do it well. But McDonald's had been missing out on another huge segment of the marketplace, people willing to pay more for breakfast, lunch, or dinner. To capture that higher end, McDonald's created a line of premium-priced items, ranging from exotic coffees and other drinks from their McCafé, to premium salads and deluxe burgers. If you want to spend $5.00 on lunch, you can get any McDonald's value meal combo. If you want to spend $10.00 on lunch, you can get their Quarter Pounder with Cheeze Deluxe and a Mocha Frappé.

Two Premium Lines

Whirlpool's line of appliances are priced in the low-to-middle range. Whirlpool also owns the Maytag brand, and its appliances are premium priced. Whirlpool also owns the Jenn-Air brand, and those appliances are super-premium priced. If you want to spend $700 on a refrigerator, you can get a Whirlpool brand. If you want to spend $1,400 on a refrigerator, you can get a Maytag. And if you want to spend $2,800+ on a refrigerator, you can get a Jenn-Air. Whichever you choose, the Whirlpool corporation makes a sale.

What Dell, McDonald's, and Whirlpool *Didn't* Do

Notice what Dell, McDonald's, and Whirlpool did not do. Dell didn't attempt to skyrocket the prices of their Dell-branded computers, McDonald's didn't attempt to surge their prices for their venerable Big Mac, fries, and soft drink. Whirlpool didn't swell the prices of their Whirlpool-branded appliances. For these brands, major price increases would have blown the low-price concept. It would have counter-acted, with potentially disastrous effect, the value image they'd meticulously built and maintained since their inception.

Instead, they created (or purchased) a whole new premium line, each with their own brand name(s) or product name(s).

Your Low End Props Up Your High End

Let's say you already have a premium, high-end line or business. In that case, you may benefit greatly by creating a lower-end, economy line or business.

The obvious advantage to doing so is to tap into that lower-end segment of the marketplace. Just like Dell, McDonald's, and Whirlpool established premium lines to tap into a segment of the marketplace they had not been serving, you who are already serving the high end can now tap into a lower end which you're not currently serving.

But the real advantage to creating an economy line or business is not as obvious. What really happens is that your newly-created lower-end line acts as a foundational support for your premium line.

Think of it this way: Without a lower-end line or business, you will live with constant temptation, or intermittent marketplace pressure, to lower your premium prices. During tough economic times, or when a competitor strikes a powerful blow, your premium line or business may just come tumbling down. But, with a lower-end line or business operating underneath, you can avoid the temptation to cheapen your premium line. If buyers suddenly shift to a lower-end preference, your premium line needn't be lowered to accommodate them because your lower-end line is already there to accommodate them.

This is the exact occurrence that caught and burnt Levi Strauss & Co. If there ever was a company in prime position to maintain a lucrative, premium-priced line, it is Levi Strauss. The man, for whom the company is named, invented the denim jean way back in the 1800s. There is nothing more American in heritage and in image (think cowboy) than Levi's jeans. And for many decades Levi's did maintain a premium position for their flagship product. But in the 1980s and '90s, pricing pressure got to them, and Levi's decided to play the low-price game (cringe). They closed their American factories and outsourced manufacturing to who-knows-where (wherever it's cheapest, turns out). Nothing like throwing your unique selling proposition — Levi's American-made image — right out the window. As a result, Levi's jeans are no longer a premium brand. Now, they're no better than any other brand. (In fact, Levi's abandonment of the high-end opened the door to other designer labels that have profited immensely by serving that segment.)

Had Levi Strauss created or purchased a lower-end brand, they could have used that brand to play the low-price game. Which would have allowed them to maintain their once-enviable position as America's premium jean at the high end.

Nike did exactly what I'm describing. A few years ago Nike bought the Converse brand of athletic shoes. Now they've got the lower-end of the marketplace covered by that brand. As a result, they can avoid any temptation to lower the lofty position, and prices, of their premium Nike line.

Here's a few other marketers known for their high-end brand that created (or purchased) a lower-end line or business for themselves:

• Giorgio Armani created a lower-end line of men's suits called the Mani brand, which is, as you would expect, priced lower than the premium Armani line. Armani also created the A/X brand of lower-priced casual clothes.

• Hallmark keeps its Hallmark brand of greeting cards premium priced, but offers two lower-priced lines (for different retailers), Connections and Expressions.

• Ann Taylor, a premium brand of women's clothing, now has Ann Taylor Loft, a lower-end chain.

• Marriott is a premium line of hotels, Courtyard and Fairfield Inn are lower-level brands owned by Marriott. And Hilton owns the lower-level Hampton Inn chain.

• Saks Fifth Avenue owns the lower-priced Off 5th outlet chain.

Your Premium Line May No Longer Be a Premium Line

You may think you have a premium line, but that may no longer be the case.

That's because a funny thing happens to premium brands over

time. Their premium polish tends to tarnish. They tend to slowly decline, over many years, to a non-premium, lower level.

This decline may or may not have anything to do with your product's inherent quality. Your quality may, in fact, be as good or better than it's ever been. Rather, it has to do with exclusiveness. For a product or service to command a premium price, it needs to be somewhat exclusive. That is, not readily available to everyone and anyone. Put another way, if everyone's got one, it's no longer special.

When credit card companies Visa, Mastercard, and American Express began price lining, they all called their premium line the "gold card." (All three using the same metallic element metaphor is an example of companies within the same industry copying one another so closely that one's idea becomes the community's idea.)

The premium gold card concept was a big hit in the credit card industry, as millions of people upgraded to gold cards. Therein laid the problem. The gold card became so ubiquitous that it lost its air of exclusivity, hence it's premium status.

Time For a New Premium Line

When your premium line is no longer all that premium, it's time to create a new premium line or even an ultra-premium line.

Since the once-premium gold credit card deteriorated to a lower level, the credit cards companies created the platinum card, anointing it the new premium.

And the same thing is happening again. I recently received a credit card solicitation in the mail inviting me to upgrade my platinum card to a titanium card.

And if you think the titanium card is the ultimate, it isn't. Most of the credit card companies have an ultra-premium card they issue, by invitation only, to only their wealthy, high-rolling customers. (The card color is black, by the way.) They keep this card out of the hands of 99.9 percent of the population, which of course, adds to the card's exclusivity, mystique, and desirability.

Gillette's New Premium Razor

Gillette has a history of creating new premium razors every few years, like clockwork. In the '90s, Gillette's Sensor was their premium men's razor. Launched with great fanfare and pizazz, it quickly became a great success. But the lifecycle of even a wildly successful razor is short, according to Gillette's playbook. So by the late '90s the Sensor was eclipsed by the newer and higher-priced Mach 3. Another round of great fanfare, great pizazz, great success. Then a few years later, they came out with the Mach 3 Turbo, followed a few years after that by the M3 Power. As this is being written, Gillette just announced the Fusion, their newest yet. By the time you read this, it's likely the Fusion will be eclipsed by yet another, higher-priced model. And another after that.

Gillette likes to follow this sequence:

1. Create a new premium razor. Price it higher than the one it will replace.
2. Market hot and heavy, especially during the launch phase. In a few years, when mass acceptance leads to eventual decline from premium to not-so premium . . .
3. Create another new premium razor at an even higher price.
4. Repeat the cycle.

Do you see the wisdom behind Gillette's strategy? Most companies lower the price when a product reaches maturity, in a attempt to keep sales aloft. Instead, Gillette raises the price by supplanting the mature razor with a newer premium model. Steadily and incrementally, they keep pushing the high end higher. (Gillette works the low end, too, with their Good News brand of disposable razor.)

To adopt a similar strategy you'd have to replace a declining product or model with a more advanced, more premium, more expensive version. Then launch it with gusto for a period of time. Seems like a great way to raise your prices and attract more business to me.

This is also an example of the Rotate Standard strategy through use of The Soda Maneuver, as described in Chapter Six. Each new razor displaces its predecessor over time, becoming the new standard.

Hibernate and Reincarnate

Another option is to discontinue a premium line or brand altogether, wait a few years, then re-introduce it at a much higher price.

Ford did this with the Thunderbird. The T-Bird was created as a premium brand, and that's exactly what it was for several years. But as I mentioned earlier, premium brands tend to decline in level over time, which is exactly what happened to the Thunderbird. Once the T-Bird had lost its premium lustre, it could no longer support a premium price. So in the late 1990s Ford just stopped manufacturing the Thunderbird altogether; took it off the market entirely. Then, several years later, they reintroduced it as a completely redesigned car, and premium priced at that. Ford did the same thing with the

Lincoln Continental. Discontinued it for several years, then re-introduced it years later at a higher price.

There's a maneuver in the financial world called the *leveraged buyout.* When a public company's stock price just isn't moving higher, and not likely to, the company is taken private. (All of its shares are bought up by a firm that specializes in this sort of thing.) Then, after a few years, the company once again goes public — at a much higher share price than what it was before. (This is how the buyout firm makes their profit.)

You don't have to let a classic brand slowly deteriorate from premium status. You may be able to revitalize your once-high-end brand by taking it off the market and letting it hibernate for a while. Then reincarnate it in a dramatically new form of some kind, at a dramatically higher price point.

What About a Service?

The Create a Premium Line or Economy Line strategy works real well for products, and it can work well for services too with some adaptation. For example, the metallic metaphor used by credit cards (silver, gold, platinum) is also popular amongst consultants and advisors who want to offer different levels of service at different price points. Even Allstate has adopted it, with both gold and platinum plans for auto insurance.

NOTE: Another great strategy for price lining services can be found in Chapter 12: Control Choice.

Alert: Flaunt Your Expensiveness.

With a premium or ultra-premium line, you want the market-place to know that particular brand is expensive. Either subtly or overtly, let the marketplace know your product is premium priced. This actually works to your advantage; it creates desire. On the other hand, if the buyer is unaware of the high price in advance, and experiences a "sticker shock" reaction when they step up to buy, your sales will suffer.

Alert: Different Line for Different People.

Most of the time, creating a premium line or economy line means you'll be targeting a different segment of the market-place with this new line. In this sense, you're not expecting your existing customers to start paying any more than they ever have. You're expecting to attract new customers who are pre-disposed to paying more.

Chapter Ten

Practice Isolation Marketing

If you sell the same way your competitors sell, distribute through the same channels as your competitors distribute, deliver the same way your competitors deliver, or locate in the same places as your competitors locate, you'll probably find it difficult to avoid competing on price. If you don't want to compete on price, then you may want to consider doing some of these things differently than your competitors. The concept is called isolation marketing.

You're Over Here, They're Over There

The idea behind isolation marketing is to avoid direct, side-by-side comparison between you and your competitors. Visualize yourself standing alone in the bright spotlight, while your numerous competitors are sitting together buried in the darkened audience. That's the concept, albeit an exaggerated analogy. The good news is you probably can achieve a level of sales, distribution, delivery, or location differences that really do isolate you from your competitors. The bad news is that the difference(s) you create may be negated in the long run, as competitors eventually copy you. The good news is that you can negate the negation, as your initial, temporary isolation may be enough to effectively launch a new product, service, or business and to gain a sustainable lead. With bold and unexpected isolation marketing at the outset, you might remain a step or two ahead and be able to maintain a higher price, even when various competitors catch on and duplicate your difference(s).

Pickles and Salad Dressing

Walk down the condiments aisle of your local grocery store and check out the pickles. More than likely, you'll see several different brands, all stacked side-by-side. But you won't find Claussen pickles there. The Claussens are in a different aisle, nowhere near the other pickle brands. Claussens are also priced considerably higher than all those other brands.

How does Claussen convince grocers to display their pickles away from the other brands? Does it take heavy-handed coercion or mammoth slotting fees? ("Slotting fees" are what manufacturers pay grocers for preferred shelf space. Paying for shelf space sounds a little underhanded, but it's a common practice in the grocery industry.) Neither. Ingeniously, Claussen makes their pickles such that they require constant refrigeration. So they end up in a refrigerated aisle, without question.

Marie's salad dressing does the same thing. You won't find Marie's with the other salad dressings because Marie's requires constant refrigeration. So where do you find Marie's in the typical grocery store? With all the refrigerated vegetables that go into salads. That's not only isolation marketing, that's ingenious marketing.

Selling Differently Than the Competition

The standard sales method most home remodelers, or contractors of any kind, use is to (a) advertise for leads, (b) cost out the projects, and (c) submit bids. Of course, that results in direct side-by-side comparison, and places emphasis on the price. Perhaps isolation marketing — which entails marketing differently than the norm in your industry — could remedy that.

Paramount Builders is a successful home remodeling company based in Virginia and spreading throughout the southeast. They specialize in vinyl siding and replacement windows. They use a completely different sales system, one that truly isolates themselves from their competitors.

Paramount Builders doesn't advertise much. Instead, they employ an army of field operatives to canvas neighborhoods, knock on doors, and set up appointments between the homeowner and company salesperson. (From the curb one can tell which houses are in need of new siding or windows, so right off the bat this move alone greatly increases the odds of finding likely prospects, logic would dictate.)

The Paramount Builders salesperson executes a thorough, well choreographed presentation in the homeowner's house, culminating in a price quote. The price includes a significant discount the buyer may earn by purchasing during this first visit, and by allowing Paramount Builders to place their sign on the front lawn during the construction project. The lawn sign then kindles subsequent sales in the neighborhood.

The homeowner gets a quality installation at a fair price, and Paramount Builders makes a sale without having to compete head-to-head based on price.

Music Sells in Isolation of Other Music

If you want to buy recorded music, you go to a music store or entertainment department of a discount store. Or perhaps you download it from a web site like iTunes. But you wouldn't go to a clothing store to buy a music CD would you? In 2003, if you wanted Madonna's latest CD you would. She and GAP entered into an arrangement whereby her then new CD would be sold exclusively at GAP stores for a certain period of time. This was isolation marketing for both Madonna and GAP, since GAP was the only place you could get Madonna's new CD, and her new CD was the only one carried by GAP.

James Taylor, Martina McBride, Elvis Presley and other singers' CDs have been offered for sale at Hallmark stores. Even some hotels and airlines have been offering CDs for sale.

Starbucks coffeehouses have been selling music CDs since the '90s, focusing on only a handful of artists each year. According to *The Wall Street Journal*, Starbucks sold over 40,000 copies of a Louis Armstrong/Duke Ellington CD in six weeks time. I guarantee you this obscure CD wouldn't have sold one tenth as much buried in the bins of traditional music stores or even online.

However, GAP, Hallmark, and Starbucks are all very selective as to which CDs they're going to carry, since they aren't going to carry very many compared to a typical music store. So, it's not simply a matter of contacting one of these companies and automatically getting your new CD in place. To put it bluntly, they may not want it. Which means this option, getting your new CD featured in GAP, Hallmark, Starbucks, or sold on some plane flight, may not be available to you.

Which brings us back to how isolation marketing actually works. The entire concept of isolation marketing is to market in ways that are not typical in your industry. If every record company got all their CDs featured at Starbucks, and Starbucks accepted them all, then that would be typical and would no longer be isolation marketing. It would no longer work for the record companies or for Starbucks. In other words, if everyone's doing it, it won't work.

Shunning Crowded Retail

When it came time to introduce their new wood cleaner and polish in the marketplace, the makers of Orange Glo knew that normal, retail sales and distribution channels would be suicidal. Competing with the likes of Procter & Gamble, Unilever, S.C. Johnson & Son and other heavyweights for coveted retail shelf space would be next to impossible. Even if they did manage to squeeze their way onto shelves they would end up having to sell at a much lower price to entice buyers to try their unknown brand.

Instead, Orange Glo went direct to the buyer, using television infomercials to create awareness, desire, and sales. The product then shipped directly to the buyer's home or office, circumventing retail distribution completely (and circumventing price comparison).

That was how they launched the product, and it worked. Orange Glo became so successful avoiding retail distribution that they eventually were able to enter retail distribution from a position of strength, allowing them to maintain their higher price even along-side competing products. Their initial isolation marketing allowed them to stay one step ahead, even when they eventually chose to market through typical channels.

My Pillow is another example. Priced around ten times higher than your typical pillow, it was sold strictly online at first, isolated from competitors. After gaining scale and muscle, it eventually ended up in retail stores, much nearer its competitors, but still able to maintain the elevated price.

It's Necessarily Different, Not Necessarily New

Shunning advertising in favor of a highly-trained salesforce, selling music CDs outside of music stores, or circumventing retail distribution in favor of direct marketing, are not new strategies. Isolation marketing does not require you to do anything new. Rather, it is simply the use of different — or opposite — marketing methods than the prevalent practices in your industry.

In this sense, isolation marketing does require different thinking on your part. If you have a contrarian mindset — if you feel comfortable trying different marketing methods when everyone says you'd be crazy to do so — you're the perfect type to practice isolation marketing.

How to Begin

Start by examining the ways of your competitors, along with the common practices in your industry. Specifically, look at the prevailing method used to sell, the prevailing method used to get the product or service into the marketplace (distribution), the prevailing way the product or service finally reaches the buyer (delivery), and the prevailing locations your competitors choose. Then design your methodologies to be significantly different in one or more of these areas.

Not Another Restaurant

As you know, restaurants tend to appear out of nowhere like pop-up ads on a web site, and then disappear into nowhere just as quickly. Many of them are forced to compete on price and end up with margins too thin to sustain operations, or they keep their prices high and end up with too few patrons to cover their fixed costs. What should a restaurant do to avoid this dilemma? Perhaps isolation marketing can help tip the odds in one's favor.

Dominic's of New York is a restaurant chain specializing in their own brand of Italian sausage, grilled with peppers and onions on Italian bread (they have a bunch of other grilled items on the menu also). Instead of locating in typical restaurant locations, Dominic's did the opposite. They have a fleet of mobile kiosks set up outside Lowe's Home Improvement stores in certain parts of the country.

I've seen this happen upon many occasions: People approach or leave a Lowe's and the irresistible aroma of grilling sausage, onions, and peppers bellowing out of the Dominic's kiosk draws them like a magnet. Instead of walking straight into the store or to their car, they suddenly make a 90-degree turn and head right for Dominic's. I know one distinguished gentleman in particular that this happens to quite often. He sets out to buy a box of screws, a wrench, or batteries and ends up eating a Dominic's hot Italian sausage in the process. In fact, this fellow has been known to visit a Lowe's store around lunch time specifically to dine at Dominic's. Once his stomach is full he then wanders into the Lowe's, since it's right there, and finds something to buy.

In most cases, like this one, isolation marketing works for all parties. Dominic's benefits and so does Lowe's. And so does the customer. Instead of driving to Lowe's to buy something and then driving somewhere else to eat, I can simply grab lunch at the Dominic's kiosk right there. I don't even have to waste time deciding what restaurant to go to, since there are no other restaurants at the Lowe's. Dominic's has that captive market all to itself.

(Again, I mention that each of these exclusive arrangements between Lowe's and Dominic's is confined to certain geographic areas. Each party is free to enter into similar deals with other parties in other geographic areas.)

Isolation or Congregation

Before we go any further, I must mention that the location aspect of isolation marketing can backfire and possibly hurt you in some situations. Sometimes, you're better off congregating right next to the competition rather than isolating yourself from them.

Ever notice that car dealers, night clubs, and hotels like to locate near one another? Even arch rivals Home Depot and Lowe's, AT&T and Verizon, and Staples and OfficeMax/Office Depot, end up locating within a short distance (in some cases a few hundred yards) of one another.

One factor you may want to consider is *decision time.* Regarding your particular product or service, if most buyers delay their purchase decision until the last moment, meaning they like to shop before deciding, you may be better off locating near the competition. Doing so accommodates the buyer's desire to compare, and places you in the thick of the action when purchase decisions are made. All other factors being equal (although they may not be equal), you'll get some of the business and your competitors will get some of the business. You each get your share of the buys at any given location.

But if most buyers of your product or service decide well in advance that they want your brand over competing brands, then you may do well isolating yourself from the competition. When people decide in advance what they want to buy, the desire to shop around is gone. Your product or service is a destination, a foregone decision.

Of course, you can hedge by practicing both isolation marketing and congregation marketing simultaneously. Orange Glo uses both infomercials (isolation marketing) and retail (congregation marketing). Dominic's has those kiosks at certain Lowe's stores (isolation) and they have some stores in mall food courts (congregation). Apple has their own stores (isolation) but also has their products in Best Buy and other retailers (congregation). I do believe that it's the isolation marketing, however, that strengthens the brand and allows it to do better in congregation settings than if congregation marketing alone was used.

From Nowhere to Gigantic

Here's three examples of how small, one-person companies grew into huge, international operations due largely to isolation marketing in their formative years.

- When Sam Walton launched Walmart, he deliberately chose to locate in small, rural towns, totally isolated from the large, entrenched department stores in large cities. In fact, it wasn't until Walmart became a thriving, multi-billion-dollar operation did they begin invading the larger cities and going head-to-head with other large competitors.

- Michael Dell founded his company in his college dorm room. He did well selling computers all by himself at first, and then hiring other salespeople. Although his modestly-growing company was quite admirable for a college kid, Dell remained a small player compared to the established computer companies in the early years. It wasn't until Dell pioneered the direct selling model using the internet that the explosive growth occurred in the 1990s and beyond.

- Selling books over the internet was a new, radical idea when Jeff Bezos created Amazon. Would Amazon have been as successful if it had been a typical brick-and-mortar bookstore instead of an internet bookstore? I doubt it. By isolating himself from all the brick-and-mortar competitors — by selling and distributing a completely different way — he achieved instant success and explosive growth.

You may have noticed that these three examples — Walmart, Dell, and Amazon — are primarily discounters, not premium pricers. Isolation marketing can be used for two different purposes. The combination of isolation marketing and discounting can produce growth on a mammoth scale, which is one purpose. If world domination is your objective, then you may be better off playing the low-price game. But since you're reading this book, we'll assume you prefer to be pricier. In that case, the combination of isolation marketing and premium pricing can produce solid, steady growth with thick profit margins, the other purpose.

Isolation Supports Price

Here are examples of isolation marketing and premium pricing.

- Snap-On Tools created a selling and distribution system quite different than the normal, retail system. Their fleet of trucks and driver/salesmen go right to professional mechanics in their work stalls. The adult version of the old Good Humor ice cream trucks, which, come to think of it, is another example of isolation marketing and premium pricing.

- Select Comfort mattresses — a.k.a. Sleep Number — uses both direct marketing and their own stores to sell premium-priced beds, isolating themselves from all the other brands lined up at bedding or department stores.

- Domino's Pizza pioneered the pizza delivery concept in the early 1960s. Ordering a pizza by phone and having it delivered to your door, rather than going to a sit-down restaurant, was a radically different sales, distribution, and delivery system when it began (and for several decades afterward).

- Kohler featured their newly-designed, premium-priced shower heads exclusively at Holiday Inn Express hotels. For Kohler, it gave them a unique and wide-spread method of exposing their new designs. For Holiday Inn Express, it gave them something special their competitors didn't have. Guests were so impressed with the shower heads that Holiday Inn Express started selling them, which benefited Holiday Inn Express, Kohler, and the buyers.

- Inside some Walmart stores you can find separately-owned service businesses, such as portrait photographers, nail salons, and income tax preparers, each with exclusivity (meaning their competitors aren't there).

- It was isolation marketing, mainly in the form of television infomercials, that launched the highly successful George Foreman, Lean, Mean, Fat-Reducing, Grilling Machine. Do you think this product would have been as successful if it simply appeared on store shelves alongside all the other grills on the market?

Repeating a point I made earlier, your isolation marketing may not be all that isolated when competitors eventually copy your methods. Isolation marketing is most prominent and effective in the early lifecycle stages of a product, service, or business. But it can still be more potent than congregation marketing no matter when it occurs. Plus, you can use competitive copycating as motivation to adopt yet another different method or methods to isolate yourself from them.

One Product Per Ad

You may want to isolate not only from your competitors, but from yourself. Quite often, you can gain market penetration and greater response by advertising just one of your products or services instead of many products or services.

Television infomercials spend 30 minutes selling just one product, even though the marketer may carry many other products as well. (They have separate infomercials for each product. They also upsell you the other products when you call or visit their website.) Print ads in newspapers and magazines usually are more effective when they feature only one product or service. Same with direct mail pieces and websites. Speaking of the latter . . .

Do you do e-commerce on the web? Certainly, you can feature all your items on your main web site. But you may also do well by establishing separate web sites for some of your products. One-product web sites can be much more successful at selling specific products than web sites which feature numerous products, especially if you want to maintain a higher price.

What about catalogs or menus? Of course, a catalog or menu wouldn't be a catalog or menu if it didn't feature a whole bunch of different products or services. That's its purpose — to give the consumer numerous items to choose from. If your catalogs, menus, or brochures are working well for you, keep them coming. But you may want to augment with some isolation marketing. You can take one product from your catalog and market it separately. Then, send your catalog to buyers of the one product.

It's a one-two punch. Use isolation marketing, in the form of one product per ad, to ferret out buyers from the population at large (or your target marketplace). Then follow-up by exposing your new customers to the other things you carry.

Alert: Are You in Position to Use Isolation Marketing?

When you sell and market directly to the end user, you are in the strongest position possible to practice isolation marketing. An example would be Apple establishing their own brick-and-mortar stores and advertising to the public at large.

When you sell wholesale to a middleman or reseller, yet market to the end user, you're in the second-best position to practice isolation marketing. An example would be Coca-Cola, advertising to the end user, but selling to bottlers/distributors, who in turn sell to retailers, who in turn sell to the consumer.

When you sell and market wholesale, and do not market to the end user, you're in the weakest position to practice isolation marketing. An example would be any industrial parts manufacturer that markets to manufacturers of various products.

Chapter Eleven

Reconfigure

My first memorable exposure to a quintessential business recon-figuration occurred way back in the 1970s.

I showed up at a barbershop for a haircut. Three months earlier (haircut frequency having been measured in months, not weeks, for twenty-two-year-olds in those days), the place was your typical barbershop. Revolving red-blue-white-striped barber pole outside, two or three middle-aged male barbers inside, the sound of electric clippers buzzing, hair piles on the floor, and a sign hanging over a mirror that read "Haircuts $3.50."

But this time, it was different. As I approached, I noticed the re-volving striped barber pole was gone. In the window was a new, large neon sign with a new name. The middle-aged, male barbers in white lab coats were gone, having been replaced by a predomi-nantly younger, predominantly female crew, all wearing pastel green polo shirts and black slacks. The owner, who used to be one of those middle-aged, lab-coated barbers himself, popped out from behind a curtain wearing black pants, black T-shirt, and black sun-glasses.

"Things have really changed around here," I remarked.

"Oh yes," the owner replied proudly. "We're not a barber shop anymore. We're a styling salon now."

And the ultimate change from barber shop to styling salon: That old "Haircuts $3.50" sign had been replaced with a new sign that read "Stylings $12.00."

There may come a time when you could elevate your gross revenue and profit margin generously by executing a reconfiguration of some kind. Maybe your entire business as a whole could benefit from a reconfiguration, or perhaps you'd like to focus on one particular product or service. This chapter will help you determine what might be right for you.

Reconfiguration vs Disruption

Before we dive in, let's make sure you and I are in sync. We'll make an important distinction between the term "reconfigure" as we're using it, and the term "disrupt," another commonly used term.

Disrupt describes a more drastic maneuver than reconfigure. An entire industry disruption is really a dismantling and reassembly, a demolition and rebuild. It's an extreme reinvention.

Reconfigure, on the other hand, describes an enhancement or improvement. It's taking an already successful product, service, or business and ratcheting it up a level or two. No demolition involved, just a good dose of revenue growth augmentation.

The Three Components of Reconfiguration

There are three main components of an effective reconfiguration: *redefine, repackage,* and *reprocedure.* By breaking it down this way, you'll be better able to get a handle on it and implement the strategy effectively.

The three components work together, so more than likely you will need at least two of the three to achieve marketplace embracement of a higher price.

Component One: Redefine

I'm sure you're familiar with most of these classic redefinitions:

Used to be:	Redefined as:
fish eggs	caviar
snails	escargot
raw fish	sushi
candy bar	energy bar
soup	stew
slimehead	orange roughy
old	classic
old junk	antique
date	social liaison
janitor	sanitation engineer
trash collection	waste management
disc jockey	air personality
replace	upgrade
day care	child development center
tie	neckware
doll	action figure

Continued . . .

Used to be:	Redefined as:
problem	issue or challenge
cameraman	photo journalist
coffee	latte
hardware store	home improvement center
junk yard	recycling emporium

Redefining your business, or a particular product or service, seems so simple. Just choose a euphemistic word or term to replace a gauche word or term. It usually isn't quite that easy, however. In fact, it can be downright tricky. That's because a good, effective redefinition must meet two tough criteria.

Your defining word or term needs to:

- **Connote some degree of exclusivity or superiority.** It could imply the exotic, élite, or adventurous. Or it could imply the technologically, ergonomically, or medicinally advanced. It could even imply seemingly negative yet oddly attractive traits like the rebellious, risqué, or dangerous. As long as it exudes an air of exclusivity and/or superiority, you're on the right track.

- **Communicate instant understanding.** The moment people see or hear your defining word or term, they need to know what it is you're all about. If it's clear and specific, it's working for you. If, on the other hand, your defining word or term is nebulous or ambiguous, it's working against you. Creating curiosity, mystique, or intrigue may be advantageous in other aspects of your marketing, but not when it comes to your defining term.

There is an exception. Your redefinement could be an esoteric word or term that people are unfamiliar with, but with which you create universal familiarity and understanding through massive exposure. The term "latte" was not commonly used until Starbucks commonly used it in their thousands of stores everywhere.

Likewise, your redefinement could be a common word or term that you use in a new way. The word "enterprise" took on a new meaning when the tech industry began using it to refer to large businesses.

You can choose a word or term that is already universally understood (the easier, safest way), or you can choose a word or term that requires you or your entire industry to create understanding (the harder, riskier way). One way or another, your defining word or term needs to be clearly, instantly understood by your target consumer if you expect them to be attracted.

Effective vs Ineffective Redefinements

The barbershop that redefined themselves as a styling salon is a perfect example of an effective redefinement. There were a few more subtle, yet important, redefinements that went along with it. "Barbers" became "stylists," "haircuts" became "stylings," and "customers" became "clients" (the latter term implying a stronger, ongoing relationship).*

Some day cares became child development centers, and that cer-

---

*Quite often, whenever you have a strong movement in one direction for a sustained period of time, a countermovement eventually springs up and grows. As a reaction to the proliferation of styling salons in the 1970s and '80s, the old-line barbershop began making a comeback in the '90s. Just last month a new barbershop opened not far from my house, complete with revolving red-blue-and-white striped pole outside.

tainly has a nice ring to it. Same with hardware stores that turned into home improvement centers.

And as one that does not care for soup and almost never eats it, I do find myself enjoying a bowl of stew from time to time. Redefinements can be most comforting.

I know a financial advisor who redefined himself as a "wealth enabler." What the heck is a wealth enabler? This term is way too ambiguous. The term financial advisor seems good enough to me, though perhaps not a home-run term.

A few years ago I bumped into a marketing consultant who decided she should drop that term and redefine herself as someone who "helps businesses succeed." While I agree that "marketing consultant" is weak and negatively-impressive in some circles, her new term is just too nebulous, too ambiguous. Any number of people help businesses succeed, including accountants, advertising agencies, information technologists, and janitors. "Helping businesses succeed" doesn't tell us what service she provides or what she actually does. Therefore, ineffective.

Several years ago a trend swept through the radio industry in which station sales representatives redefined themselves as "marketing consultants," under the presumption that "marketing consultant" would connote a more statuesque position than the relatively minor "sales representative." (It may not be an improvement, but that was the thinking at the time.) This term even appeared on their business cards below their names. While we can't begrudge anyone from bettering themselves through redefinition, there is a glaring problem here. The fact is, these people weren't marketing consultants at all. They were salespeople, plain and simple. This redefinition actually ended up hurting their credibility in the business community because it was obvious they were attempting to portray themselves as something other than what they really were. The lesson: If a defining term isn't accurate, don't use it.

You can, however, embellish somewhat. Redefinement — with an embellishing flair — has swept through the restaurant industry, especially when it comes to entrée description. Ham and cheese sandwiches are now croque-monsieur, tuna with mayonnaise became salade niçoise, and fried fish is called sole menuire. Over the top, perhaps (unless you're French, in which case they'd all seem normal). But they work. Hey, if I'm going to spend big, I want a dinner that sounds exotic and unique. (Somehow, an exotically-named dish tastes better. Same way a sparkling-clean car runs better.)

Redefining This Book

I could have fallen into the nebulous definement trap with this book. I could have defined it simply as a "sales and marketing" book. Accurate but ambiguous. But since the book deals with one aspect of sales and marketing, pricing, I exploited that angle and redefined it as "The Pricing Power Playbook" and used that as the subtitle. The term "pricing power" is widely used in business as a reference to the raising of prices, so it carries with it instant understanding and desirability. "Playbook" refers to the master game plan used by sports teams, and connotes an air of wisdom. The alliteration was simply a bonus.

The title of this book is another matter. Raising prices and attracting more business are somewhat contradictory concepts, and my combination of the two in the title produces some mystique and intrigue, which is desirable in this instance.

Component Two: Repackage

Let's use the term "package" to mean the physical form of the product and/or the container it comes in. Let's extend the definition to include intangible services, in which case "package" refers to the appearance of related tangibles, such as printed sales materials, the service provider's building or office, the wardrobe or appearance of people providing the service, etc.

When you repackage, you're altering one or more aspects of your package in ways that buttresses a price increase.

More Convenience, Higher Price

For decades, Campbell's soup came in standard 10.75-ounce metal cans. They still do, in fact. As I mentioned earlier, I'm not much of a soup fan, but if I'm going to eat soup it's got to be the tomato flavor. (Regarding any kind of food, if it's got tomato in it, I'm sure to like it.)

I saw a bunch of these Campbell's tomato soup cans on my local grocery store's shelves the other day, priced at 79 cents each. On a shelf to the right of all these metal soup cans is a plastic can version. Same manufacturer, Campbell's. Same flavor, tomato. Same 10.75-ounce size in fact. Only these plastic cans were priced at $1.49 each. Seventy cents more for the same thing in a plastic can versus a metal can. (Actually, the metal can version requires dilution with water, resulting in considerably more than 10.75 ounces of consumable product. Whereas the plastic can version isn't dilutable, and makes no more than the existing 10.75 ounces. So you get a lot more to eat with the cheaper metal cans than you do with the more expensive plastic cans.)

Campbell's has created a way to raise the price of their good old tomato soup by a whopping 88 percent, simply by repackaging.

Why would anyone buy the plastic can version if it's that much more? Did I mention that the plastic can is microwavable? In fact, these plastic soup cans are designed specifically to be microwaved. Then, using the specially designed lid, you drink the soup like a cup of coffee. Campbell's calls it "Soup at Hand." Seems a little shameful to admit this, with all the starving people in the world, but opening a metal can, de-clumping and diluting the product, standing over the stove for several minutes stirring, is way too much trouble for me. Just not going to happen. But shoving the plastic can version into the microwave and drinking it 75 seconds later is perfect. Another example of the consumer gladly paying more because they get more. In this case the "more" is convenience and the saving of time, not more product.

Frito-Lay's Doritos come in a 13-ounce bag. A repackaged version comes in a 2.625-ounce can. The can version is called Mini Doritos because they're smaller than the bag version. Compared ounce-for-ounce, the smaller chips in the smaller can cost 139 percent more than the larger chips in the larger bag. Lots less product for lots more money. The benefit to Frito-Lay is a major bump-up in revenue and margin with the can version; the benefit to the consumer is a major bump-up in convenience. (The can is less spillable than the bag and fits into most automobile drink holders.)

Here are more examples of highly effective repackages:

• Time-Life repackages old songs in themed CD sets such as "Love

Songs of the '70s," "Classic Soul Ballads," "Superstars of Country," "Rock Legends," and the like. Remember, the songs are not new creations; they're the same old songs originally recorded decades ago. But Time-Life repackages the old songs in newly-created "collections." The repackage results in a whole new, promotable product, even though the content is not new.

- I priced watermelons at my local grocery store the other day. Here's what I found: A whole watermelon, weighing 16 pounds even (I know because I bought it and weighed it), cost $4.99. This equals 31.2 cents per pound. Cut watermelon, in one-quarter or one-eighth pieces, cost 49 cents per pound. Cut even further into bite-sized pieces and packaged in a plastic container, cost $1.66 per pound.

   Conclusion: The grocery store has raised the price of watermelon significantly through nothing other than repackaging. Remember, the melon itself is unchanged. Watermelon is watermelon. The only thing that changed, other than the price, is the way it's packaged.

- Let's say I offered to sell you 32 one-dollar bills for $50. You hand me $50 and I hand you $32 in return, nothing more to it. Does that sound good? Would you take me up on that deal?

   Well, the U.S. Bureau of Engraving and Printing offers exactly that deal to the public and the public buys each and every day. The only thing I hadn't mentioned is that the 32 one-dollar bills they sell you for $50 aren't cut apart like regular bills. All 32 are on one large sheet, as they are when they come off the printing press. These 32-bill sheets aren't even the finished product since they haven't been cut into single bills yet. But the clever repackagement makes the large sheet of bills a finished product, and allows them to be sold for a 56-percent premium.

- Oreo cookies now come in various configurations other than the traditional. You can get Oreo Minis, about the size of a nickel, or even Oreo Fun Stix which are long, rolled up wafers. These other, non-traditional versions, are priced considerably above the traditional versions.

- Here's one that relates to a business that I'm in, information marketing. Using average prices to illustrate, consider this:

    A paperback book sells for $14. The exact same information in a hardcover book sells for $24. The exact same information printed on 8.5x11-size paper and spiral bound, and redefined as a "manual" instead of "book," sells for $35. The exact same information, divided into sections and bound in a handsome three-ring binder, sells for $70. And the exact same information, in the three-ring binder, augmented with audio CDs or DVDs (which may contain additional information), along with any number of other whistles or bells, and redefined as a "system," can sell for $200, $300, $500, or up. The repackagement, combined with some redefinment, is what allows higher prices to prevail.

Component Three: Reprocedure

Would a different method, a different system, or a different set of sequential steps improve your operation? Would a different way of doing things add to the value you provide to your customers?

When you dream up new ways of doing things and implement them you are reproceduring.

Some reprocedures can be internal and not readily visible to buyers (although they will likely see the result of it). For example, the founders of The Home Depot reprocedured the way all that merchandise gets into the stores to begin with. They initiated the practice of buying directly from manufacturers instead of from wholesalers or distributors. This was a radical departure from the traditional, ingrained system where middlemen were well established in the industry. It was not easy bucking the system, but acceptance of their reprocedure grew in time, to where the entire home improvement industry now operates primarily direct from manufacturer to retailer.

Some reprocedures center around the way the merchandise is purchased and/or delivered, therefore readily apparent to the buyer. For example, Costco, Sam's Club, and BJ's Wholesale have reprocedured in a number of ways, relative to traditional retail methods. They require the buyer pay a membership fee to join, which then entitles the buyer to realize otherwise unattainable discounts. This also translates into different in-and-out procedures. On your way in, you have to flash your membership card to get past the door guard. And on your way out, you are offered no bags in which to carry your purchases. (They do offer you old merchandise cartons, and why not? They were only going to throw them out anyway.)

It may seem to you that the reprocedures I've just described, such as Home Depot buying directly from manufacturers, or Costco, Sam's Club, and BJ's Wholesale charging an up-front membership fee, are anything but new or innovative. They may seem inconsequential to you because they've been in effect for many years now and you've grown accustomed to them. But when they first appeared, they were quite revolutionary. Your reprocedures may only be new or innovative for a short period of time, but that is enough. As long as they're an improvement of some kind, newness (or lack of it) isn't an issue.

Reproceduring for Premium Pricing

For discounters, the goal of any reprocedure is to lower prices (or at least keep them in check). Customers understand this, and are usually willing to accept lower quality, less convenience, or less service in exchange for saving money. That's why no one complains about a lack of bags at Costco or Sam's Club. For discounters, reproceduring for less customer convenience can work (to a point).

For premium pricers, the goal of any reprocedure is to provide some form of "more" so as to justify a higher price. Usually, no one thing will do the trick. It may require several small things. Remember our discussion of the Great Customer Experience back in Chapter Two? We said that the secret to a great or greater customer experience is really a bunch of small details that collectively add up to a lot. Same is true here. In fact, the two concepts are linked in that reproceduring is a great way to create a greater customer experience.

Your objective is to create and implement better systems and procedures that raise the level of "more" you provide. The "more" can be better quality of product or service. It can be more attentive, personalized service. It can be more convenience or faster response. Examples would include Enterprise Rent-a-Car that reprocedured car rental by picking you up at your home or business with the rental car instead of you having to go to them, and the Brew-Thru beer store that reprocedured beer purchasing by loading the beer in your car as you drive through. Or the dentist that schedules appointments at 6am. Or Amazon Prime with two-day — or even one-day — delivery.

Now it's your turn. Think of ways to reprocedure, with a goal of providing greater convenience, faster speed, or some other advantage, to the buyer. People will pay more to get more, especially when you save them time and trouble.

Alert: Tough is Good.

Reconfiguring may involve some major changes in your physical facility, your internal structure, or the way you market. It may not be easy to make these changes. Remember this: If it's tough for you to do, it's at least that tough for your competitors to duplicate. Ideally, your reconfiguration would be (or would appear to be) so tough to do that no competitor considers copying you. Or if they do attempt a duplication they make too many mistakes to ever catch up with you.

Chapter Twelve

Control Choice

You may be questioning whether you should raise your prices or not. Perhaps you shouldn't. Instead, why not let your customers raise your prices for you?

This can happen when you give them the choice of paying what they're currently paying or paying more. When the offer is made correctly, your customers will choose to pay more a good percentage of the time. The secret is based on the venerable choice principle.

Choice is Sacrosanct

The freedom to choose is one of the most revered principles upon which the United States of America and other democratic nations are founded. Since the freedom to choose how to live is probably the most valued of our inalienable rights, we fight with everything we've got to keep it that way whenever our freedom comes under attack. It's supremely important.

The freedom to choose is no more vivid each and every day, as people in a capitalist, free enterprise society choose how they spend their money. They can buy from you or they can buy from your competitors. Or they can choose not to buy at all. The choice remains the consumer's; he or she is free to spend their money however they like.

Always Protect The Buyer's Right to Choose

Whatever you do, don't take away the consumer's right to choose. Don't challenge it or even allude to any choice limitation.

I once saw a billboard for a real estate brokerage that brazenly announced that they were "Your Only Choice." If their intent was to make people cringe, to activate spite, and to cause outright hostility, they certainly succeeded with that dumb declaration.

On the other hand, AT&T's classic slogan "The Right Choice" was wonderful. (They haven't used it in years, probably because it's not necessarily true. But it worked well at the time.) So are lines like "Thank you for choosing XYZ Cleaning." Anything that demonstrates your respect for the buyer's right to choose is golden.

Choice is The Brain's Favorite Exercise

Preceding every purchase is a decision to make that purchase. In other words, the buyer exercises her right to choose by selecting the product, service, or company, then acts in the chosen manner by making the purchase. The brain likes to choose, and will do so before each purchase decision (with two exceptions, explained below). We'll refer to this ritual as the *choice exercise.*

The Two Exceptions

Sometimes the buyer's brain doesn't go through the choice exercise before deciding to purchase. This happens under either of these conditions:

- **Someone else has made the purchase decision.** The buyer was merely instructed to make the purchase by a "shadow buyer" — the real decision maker lurking somewhere back in the shadows — who has gone through the choice exercise and made the buy decision. Note however that you, the marketer, may not have any direct contact with the shadow buyer or may not even know of that person's existence. (Sometimes the buyer will be reluctant to admit that they are merely an executor and not the actual decision maker.)

- **A buying habit is in effect.** The buyer makes a purchase out of habit, without going through the choice exercise. Actually the choice exercise and subsequent buy decision did happen, but that was some time earlier, perhaps weeks, months, or even years ago. Subsequently, the buyer makes purchases of a particular brand of product or service at regular intervals without re-choosing before hand. Like when you go to the same restaurant on the same day of the week, sit at the same table, and order the same meal, without questioning it all.

Having acknowledged these two exceptions, we'll now ignore them. To keep this discussion simple and usable, we'll assume the buyer's brain does go through the obligatory choice exercise before each purchase decision. The Control Choice strategy is just easier to implement this way. Once you've implemented the strategy and have it working for you, you can then take either of these two exceptions into account and adjust accordingly.

Controlling The Choices

Why not control the number or type of options that the buyer can choose from, rather than relinquishing that control to the marketplace? Why not set things up in such a way that the buyer is more likely to choose to buy from you instead of your competitor? Why not set things up in such a way that the buyer chooses to pay more, by choosing a higher-priced option, instead of considering a cheaper price from somewhere else?

The technique is called Control Choice. And before I explain how it works, let me first clarify just how I'm using the word "control" here. I'm not suggesting we attempt to commandeer buyers' brains and manipulate their decisions. Any attempt to manipulate, even if it could be achieved, is not in anyone's best interest. We marketers recognize that the consumer is in charge and free to purchase whatever he or she wants. But I am suggesting we control the available choices in such a manner that increases the likelihood the consumer will choose to buy from us, at the preferred price we want to sell for.

What "Flavor" Do You Want?

When Apple introduced their second generation of iMac computers in 1999, they made them available in five different colors. They called them "flavors." You could get your iMac in Tangerine (orange), Lime (green), Grape (purple), Raspberry (red), or Blueberry (blue). Apple continues to do a similar thing with the iPhone, giving the buyer a choice as to color.

Industry observers seemed to brush off this multi-color array as nothing more than a cute stunt only twelve-year-olds would appreciate. They failed to see the true brilliance of Apple's multi-color offering. What Apple did was control choice. They set things up so that when the buyer's brain went through the obligatory choice exercise, Apple won no matter what the decision. The choice exercise was no longer about brand, as in "What brand of smart phone should I get?" but rather it was about color, as in "What color iPhone should I get?"

And, it should be noted, the iPhone tends to be priced somewhat higher than comparable brands. (Apple generally maintains a richer pricing structure, which bolsters their artsy, élite image and therefore probably works to their advantage. But, as it turns out, when you compare quality and features, including the operating system and apps that come free with Apple devices, it turns out Apple is quite often cheaper than competing brands.)

The Objective

With the Control Choice strategy, your objective is twofold. One, you want to offer the buyer a few different options, so that choosing among your options fulfills the buyer's need to exercise choice, thus averting the need to consider other options that don't include buying from you. Two, you want all your options to not only lead to a sale for you, but at your desired price.

There are two different ways of controlling choice. Since we've already begun discussing Apple's way, let's continue with that method.

The One Variable, One Price Method

With the iPhone line, Apple offers different colors of product. Color is the only variable. Other than color, the specs are exactly alike. (Apple does have different product versions based on spec differences, but that's not what I'm talking about here.) The point: Apple's method of controlling choice is to change only one variable, color.

Here's some other examples:

• Oreck offers their flagship vacuum cleaner in black, yellow, and red. Same specs, just different colors.

• Whilrpool's refrigerators (and other products) come in white, black, and stainless steel silver.

• Beats headphones. Same specs, different colors. (Beats is owned by Apple. No coincidence they market the same way.)

• Mr. Clean antibacterial cleaner comes in four different scents, one for each season. There's Spring Garden, Summer Citrus, Sparkling Apple, and Invigorating Breeze.

With the One Variable, One Price method of controlling choice, your price stays the same across variables. You can choose which color of iPhone, Oreck, or refrigerator you like, but you pay the same price no matter which one you choose.

Can you use a variable other than color? Absolutely. Use any one variable you like, as long as there isn't a price difference among them. Mr. Clean uses scent as the variable. Coca-Cola uses flavor, offering you Coca-Cola Classic, Coca-Cola with Lime, Cherry Coke, and Black Cherry Vanilla Coke.

You might use a different design as your variable. From time to time TV Guide magazine will produce the same issue but with different covers. Different cover designs for the same issue is like multiple doors that all lead to the same room. The buyer goes through the choice exercise, settles on a cover, and buys TV Guide.

Several years ago Garth Brooks did the same thing by releasing the same CD with four different cover designs.

There is another interesting result of the One Variable, One Price method that sometimes happens. People may choose to buy more product, more often.

TV Guide discovered that a surprising number of people bought all of the cover designs of the same issue. And I'll bet you know someone who owns more than one version of that Garth Brooks CD.

Before, you only needed one bottle of Mr. Clean. But since seasons change, now you need four different bottles. A friend of mine bought a white Apple HomePod . . . then bought a black one a month later. "I liked both colors," he explained, "so I bought them both."

The Good-Better-Best Method

Electronics retailers sometimes offer a particular product in three different versions, categorizing them as "good," "better," and "best." It's a three-choice array of similar products with some spec differences.

With this method, your price ascends as the quality and/or quantity ascends. If a buyer wants the lowest-price version, fine. But more often than not, they'll choose either the middle-priced version or the highest-price version.

Here's a few examples:

• Go to the toy department of your favorite retailer or Amazon and check out the Monopoly game. You can get the Classis version for around $15, the Deluxe Vintage version for $90, or the Luxury version for $220. This good-better-best method of controlling choice is a great way to raise the price, and sell more, of an old game that might otherwise be long forgotten.

• Duracell gives you two choices: their regular Coppertop battery or their longer-lasting, higher-priced Ultra battery.

• The original Twilight Zone television series is available on DVD, in four different versions. There's the low-end version with individual episodes on single disks, a boxed-set version, a Gold Collection version with some bonus material, and The Definitive Edition with remastered video and even more bonus material. Keep these three points in mind: (1) Each of these Twilight Zone

DVD versions is really the same old material just repackaged, (2) each successive version is more expensive than the previous version, and (3) consumers overwhelmingly choose the higher-priced versions.

The Good-Better-Best Method works equally well for services as well as products.

Comcast and other cable companies offer varying levels of service for different monthly rates. Car washes offer varying levels of clean and shine for different prices.

Let's say you're in the security business, and a prospect asks you to submit a price quote for providing security services for a high-rise office complex. Remember, the brain wants to exercise choice before making a buy decision. So if you only submit one price, the customer will feel compelled to get one or two other price quotes from which to choose — and those others will be from your competitors. Assuming the customer gets three price quotes, you have a 33.3 percent chance of getting chosen. But if you submit a quote with three different options — different specs at different prices — you have a much greater chance of being chosen, and at a higher price to boot (when they choose one of your high-priced options).

This Good-Better-Best Method of controlling choice is different than what we talked about in Chapter 9: Create a Premium Line or Economy Line. They appear to be similar, but are really different in one important way. When you have three different lines of product — an economy line, a standard line, and a premium line, let's say — you're most likely marketing each line to different segments of the marketplace. Different product lines for different people. But when you control choice using the Good-Better-Best method, you're offering these three options to the same segment of the marketplace. The same consumer is exposed to all three options and is asked to choose among them.

How Many Options?

There's another dimension to all of this I've only alluded to thus far, and it's time to address it in greater detail. The Control Choice strategy involves you offering an array of options from which the buyer may choose. The question is, how many options should you offer? Three? Five? Ten? Twenty-five? Seventeen thousand?

With both the One Variable, One Price method and the Good-Better-Best method, the optimum number of options is two, three, four, or five.

If you offer more than five options, you risk creating a bigger problem. I stated several times that the brain likes to go through the choice exercise before making a buy decision. That's true if the choice is relatively easy. But if choosing amongst variables becomes difficult, the brain avoids making a decision altogether. And the more variables from which to choose, the more difficult it is to decide.

Before the proliferation of cable and satellite television, most cities had only three or four television channels available to watch. Back then it seemed people had no trouble choosing which one to watch, and they seemed pleased with their decision. Now, we've got 170, or 340, or 559, or however many channels from which to choose, and people just keep clicking through, unable to decide, and not particularly happy with what they eventually do end up watching.

There is an exception. You can offer an unlimited number of options, provided you supply expert guidance and advice as part of the sales process. For example, a carpeting retailer might offer hundreds of options, based on combinations of manufacturer, wearability, style, color, size, etc. But they'd better be set up to provide knowledgeable guidance, and a lot of hand holding, if they want the prospect to buy instead of wander away in a daze.

Bonus Points for Creativity

With the One Variable, One Price Method and the Good-Better-Best Method, I've presented you with two highly-structured ways to control choice. This should make things fairly easy to implement.

But you can get creative and control choice in other ways. A great example is Select Comfort's Sleep Number mattress. Their celebrity endorsers focus on the "sleep number" angle, each revealing his or her preferred sleep number and asking "what sleep number are you?" The choice is centered around the sleep number, not on what brand of mattress to buy. Providing the brain with this sleep number choice diverts it from focusing on brand choice. Like feeding chicken to alligators so the gators won't eat your leg.

If you feel the creative juices flowing, I'll end this chapter now and let you get to it. Just make sure you accomplish either of these two objectives: Your option array should engage the buyer (provide their brain with enticing choice exercise food, in other words) to divert them from choosing amongst competing brands. Or, your choices should include higher-priced versions to allow the buyer the option of spending more money.

Alert: No Alert.

There are no known side effects of the Control Choice strategy. Go for it.

Chapter Thirteen

Restrict Supply

Ah, yes. The old law of supply and demand. It always boils down to this, it seems.

Please allow me, without fear of accusation for insulting your intelligence or that of the many noble scholars who devote their lives to economic complexity, to summarize Econ 101 in two sentences. The price at which something sells is the intersection of the demand and supply curves. Thus, we have two variables to work with to affect price: demand and supply. (Not counting the other variables outside the law of supply and demand, as delineated in the other chapters of this book.)

You could, as a marketer, do all kinds of things to create demand. In fact, I've already written an entire book about this.* Now, it's time to address the supply side of the equation.

Meeting Demand

Econ 101, along with simple logic (economics and logic are not always in opposition, you know), also tells us that if you want to

---

Creating Demand by Rick Ott.

make the most amount of sales revenue, you should meet demand. If 1,000 consumers with fists full of cash are willing to slam their money onto the table in exchange for your whatchamacallit, then you obviously produce 1,000 whatchamacallits and make the sales. If ten times that number of consumers — 10,000 — are demanding your whatchamacallit, you produce 10,000 units and pocket ten times the revenue.

Meeting demand — that is, adjusting supply to match buyers' desire to purchase — is so logical, in fact, that economists call it "equilibrium." "When the amount offered just equals the amount demanded at a particular price," you're in equilibrium — exactly where you're supposed to be. And like water that seeks its own level, the marketplaces' natural tendency is to seek equilibrium, economists tell us.

The business press is quick to chastise a company when it fails to meet demand. They'll say a particular company is having "supply problems" or "operational breakdowns" by having order backlogs, especially when new products are introduced. How could the bumbleheads at XYZ Company have "misjudged demand" so poorly?, the press will rhetorically speculate.

Yet we notice these same out-of-equilibrium companies are able to maintain relatively high prices over long periods of time, under varying levels of demand. Could it be that not meeting demand is a good thing, assuming a company wants to sell at a higher price?

If You Want to Maintain Price, Don't Meet Demand

Meeting demand is the fastest way to deflate your prices. If you want to maintain a high price, you've got to maintain an imbalance between demand and supply, where demand exceeds supply.

Out of Equilibrium

Why does Disney take their videos off the market for years at a time? ("On January thirty-first, all three Lion King movies go back in the Disney vault," a recent television commercial announced.) If Disney kept the Lion King DVD (or any other title) on store shelves indefinitely, they'd then be forced to keep those units selling. Which would inevitably lead to discounting the price. What's the best way to avoid discounting? Limit supply. There's zero pressure to move the product when the product isn't on the market. By restricting the supply of DVDs from time to time, Disney not only avoids the pressure to discount, but they allow demand to rebuild, which fosters a whole new wave of sales when the DVDs reappear a few years later.*

Why doesn't Harley-Davidson build another factory or two so buyers don't have to wait months to take delivery of a new bike? Meeting demand would result in higher sales and higher profits, it would seem. In reality, that's exactly what would happen — in the short run. But in the long run, meeting demand would result in lower prices, lower revenue, and lower profits. If Harley-Davidson met demand, all it would take is one small slowdown in demand for a glut of bikes to suddenly accumulate in dealer showrooms. Plus, there would be pressure to keep the factories running, resulting in an ever-widening demand-supply imbalance in the wrong

---

*Over the top services like Disney+ make titles available upon demand, but then you pay a monthly subscription fee for that availability (and you don't own the DVD).

direction. This is what happens to auto makers all the time, forcing them to lower prices, offer rebates, offer zero-interest financing, offer employee discounts to anyone, whatever, just to keep the oversupply moving.

Leaving Money on the Table

There is a common sentiment that runs like this: If you don't have product available to sell when the buyer is ready to buy, they'll buy from a competitor who does have product available. Put another way, the buyer is going to buy when they're ready to buy, and if you don't sell to them, someone else will. If you restrict supply, you end up forfeiting revenue by not being in the game.

Does this reasoning make sense? Of course it does — for a marketer willing to sell at low prices. This, after all, is the thinking behind the big-box discount retailers that are open 24/7 with merchandise stacked to the ceiling. Whenever anyone is ready to spend some money, they're ready to collect it.

But this reasoning may not be best for a marketer intent on keeping their prices high.

To continue with the above two examples, if mom wants to purchase a DVD for her child, and the one she prefers from Disney isn't available, she'll simply buy a different video. Let's just say it's from a studio other than Disney, which is entirely possible. Disney then loses out on that sale. They forfeit some sales in exchange for keeping their prices high (when the product is available).

If you walk into a Harley-Davidson dealership and they tell you there's a waiting list for the model you want, you could buy another model or go somewhere else and buy another brand. In the latter instance, when a consumer buys a Triumph, Kawasaki, Suzuki, Honda, or any other brand, Harley-Davidson has lost that sale. And in exchange for forfeiting some sales (by not opening new factories so as to meet demand), they're able keep prices where they want them.

Consider what Nike did in 2003. They pulled their hottest selling Nike brand shoes out of Foot Locker stores, the world's biggest shoe retailer. According to published reports at the time, Nike didn't like the fact that Foot Locker was discounting their shoes. Nike tends to dictate rather tough terms to the retailers it supplies, and Foot Locker was deviating from those conditions. So Nike "cut them off," as it was described. Nike would rather forgo sales volume to maintain price and margin. Although, in this particular instance, Nike was eventually able to replace the lost Foot Locker sales with other retailers, and has since reconciled with Foot Locker.

Then in 2005, Nike pulled their flagship brand out of Sears stores. Since Sears had just merged with Kmart, Nike wanted to eliminate the possibility that their Nike-branded goods would end up in Kmart, a discounter. Nike also pulled their Tiger Woods golf shirts out of department stores, making them available only in pro shops or speciality stores.

Nike, Disney, Harley-Davidson, and other veterans of the premium-price game are willing to leave money on the table from time to time. They restrict supply to maintain price and margin.

To Restrict Supply or Not

Here's the bottom line:

If it drives you crazy, makes you sweat, hyperventilate, and boil with anger when the customer buys from someone else, then you may be better off playing the low-price game. In which case you need to have product or services available whenever the buyer is ready to buy, and be prepared to cut your prices whenever necessary to make every potential sale.

On the other hand, if it drives you crazy to compete on price, makes you sweat, hyperventilate, and boil with anger to see your margins shrink, then you're better off playing the high-price game. In which case you may need to restrict supply and be content leaving some money on the table from time to time.

Restrict the Time Available to Buy

There are three main ways to restrict supply: *time, unit,* and *space.*

The previous mention of Disney pulling their DVDs off the market from time to time is an example of restricting supply based on time. Sometimes a title is for sale, sometimes it isn't. If the buyer wants one of these videos, they'd better buy while the video is available — and pay the asking price — or they'll soon be out of luck. Fast food restaurants do this too, when a particular item is available "for a limited time only," and it disappears from the menu when the time period runs out.

As a consumer, has this ever happened to you? You see something you really want, and have every intention of purchasing, but you hold off in search of a lower price. Subsequently one of two things happens. One possible scenario is that you do indeed find the item somewhere else at a lower price, or in time the item's price is reduced. The other possible scenario is that the item disappears from the market and is no longer available, at any price. It's this latter scenario that has you kicking yourself for not grabbing the item when you had the chance. In retrospect, your hesitation to buy when you had the chance appears regrettable. You wish you'd have paid the price and owned the item.

As a marketer, how would you like consumers to act? If you want them to argue price or wait until you lower your price before they buy, then keep your product or service available all the time. If you want them to buy quickly at your asking price, and feel fortunate they got it, then pull the product or service off the market for periods of time. You educate, or condition consumers to pay premium prices, by restricting supply with some regularity.

"Limited time only" offers act as a price support. It's simply a method of keeping the demand-supply scale imbalanced, or to use the economist's term, out of equilibrium.

To be clear, I'm talking about maintaining price and limiting the time that the product or service is available. I'm not talking about lowing the price, putting it on sale, and putting a time limit on that. Not that putting something on sale isn't a valid strategy, it's just not this restrict supply strategy.

Restrict the Number of Units Available

The Harley-Davidson example above, where they produce less bikes than the number demanded, is an example of restricting supply based on units. They only produce so many per month of a particular model, and if you want one, you'd better add your name to the waiting list and be willing to pay the asking price, or you're out of luck.

I also mentioned earlier that auto makers tend to do the opposite. They attempt to meet demand and thus end up discounting to move the oversupply. (Meeting demand will always result in an oversupply because demand declines when buyers get what they want. You no longer are in the market for a new vehicle once you buy the new vehicle.) Auto makers have, however, restricted units at times, and it seems to work. I have a friend that owns a 1994 limited-edition Mustang convertible. It even has a fraction-type marking under the hood indicating that this car is number such-and-such from a total production run of such-and-such, much like artists number their prints. As a consequence, the car sold for top-dollar new, and my friend tells me she's been offered almost as much for it recently.

"While supplies last," or "limited edition" offers act as a price support. It's another way to maintain your demand-outbalances-supply environment, using units as the variable.

Restrict the Space Available

New York City. Lots of people crammed into a relatively small geo-graphic area. Space limitations abound in New York, which results in more demand than supply and thus disproportionately high prices for just about everything.

Some restaurants in NYC are so busy you can't get in. You can't even get on the reservation list. There seems to be a whole lot more demand than supply, resulting in very high menu prices. But let's say one of these restaurants was able to double or triple their physi-cal size, thus accommodating many more customers. What would happen? In the short run, all those people who previously couldn't get a reservation would now get a reservation, and the restaurant would see a big spike in their gross sales and net income. In the short run, the expansion would look like a brilliant move.

But in the longer run (which might only be a few weeks in the restaurant business), the supply/demand balance would begin to work against the establishment. With reservations easy to get, people would no longer be motivated to expend much time and energy getting them. They wouldn't feel special or privileged when they did get them. And they certainly wouldn't expect to pay top dollar for a meal that's readily available to anyone who walked in off the street. At the same time, the restaurant would feel pressure to fill the available tables, which would inevitably result in discounting.

A few months ago a new, high-end restaurant opened in my home town. After a friend and his current inamorata dined there the previous weekend, I asked him how he liked the place.

"Too expensive," he replied. "The food's overpriced, the drinks are overpriced. We're not going back."

Assuming his assessment is shared by others, what conclusion would you draw from that? Would you say this restaurant is charging too much, delivering too little value, or both? I'd say the place must be too easy to get into.

So I checked it out myself recently, and found a big problem right off the bat, before the prices or food quality even came into play. First off, my date and I walked right in; no reservations were necessary (this was a Friday night at 7pm, at the height of dinner time). It was very large; lots of undivided square footage. And about half the tables were empty. All bad signs.

The problem is, this place is just too big. It will therefore remain too easy to get into and will always have too many empty tables. Conditions not conducive to high prices.

What should the owners do? As I see it, there are only two alternatives (assuming going out of business is unacceptable). Either a drastic lowering of the prices, thus becoming a bargain restaurant rather than a high-end restaurant. Or, restrict space by dividing the place in half, creating two entirely different restaurants (they could have a common kitchen), one high-end and the other moderately priced. And elevate the floor a few feet above street level. (This floor thing is a different strategy entirely and outside the perimeters of this book. But it does work, so I thought I'd throw it in.)

Here are a few more examples:

- In the spring of 2005, George Lucas released a new Star Wars movie. In Los Angeles, where the movie first premiered, people began waiting in line at a movie theater over a month before the premiere! And they were willing to pay whatever the ticket price just to get in and be one of the first to see the movie. Do you think these Star Wars fans would be as willing to spend their time and money this way if the movie were debuting at every theatre in town instead of just one? They might still be excited to see the movie, but they wouldn't camp out for a month in advance at a theatre and pay whatever it took to get a seat. It's the limited number of seats, or space available, that creates the demand/ supply imbalance, which renders price a non-issue.

- Universities that limit enrollment, thus ensuring there will always be more applicants than space available, are the ones with the highest tuition. They also make applicants jump through all kinds of hoops to be "considered" for "acceptance."
  Universities with plenty of room are the ones with much lower

tuition. Some have even had to lower standards and actively recruit students, all because they want to fill the space available.

• There's a 30-year waiting list to buy tickets to Green Bay Packers home football games, regardless of whether the team is winning or losing. That's a whole lot more demand than supply, which keeps ticket prices high. A few years ago they renovated Lambeau Field and made it a little larger. But there's still much more demand than available seats, so it still works. But if it were possible to double or triple the stadium's size, the entire picture would change. Practically everyone who wanted tickets could get them (Green Bay is not a large city), the excitement of attaining something rare would be gone, delight would dwindle, there'd be empty seats at every game, and ticket prices would crash.

The Space Restriction Bonus

When you restrict the space available, you create another interesting condition. Physical space limitations tend to produce a heightened sense of togetherness, camaraderie, and bonding. Thus vacationers on cruise ships — a confined environment — feel a heightened sense of intimacy even amongst strangers. Same phenomenon in smaller restaurants and night clubs. Or offices and boardrooms where negotiations take place. Or any slightly confining space (though people need to be free to leave whenever they want).

Once again, it's the subconscious mind at work here. Logically, people may be attracted to the big restaurant, big night club, big cruise ship, or big meeting room. What they don't consciously realize is that they actually end up enjoying the smaller places better, due to the increased intimacy.

Large, cavernous, opulent hotels are the rage in Las Vegas. But they discovered that many of their guests prefer not to gamble in those huge casinos, opting instead for much smaller settings elsewhere. If you have a large physical facility, an option may be to subdivide it into smaller, more intimate settings.

Togetherness, camaraderie, and intimacy are rare and valuable things, most of the time. They can add to the price people are willing to pay to be part of that limited space environment.

Alert: Not Recommended for Necessities or Monopolies.

If you have a monopoly or an oligopoly, or produce a product or service needed for the sustenance of life, or in emergencies, do not restrict supply. Examples would be energy, utilities, medicine, medical services, disaster relief supplies, basic food items. Restricting supply only works in a competitive environment when the consumer has other options readily available.

Paperback; 250 pages
ISBN: 0-9663491-1-3
$22. U.S. $30. CANADA

Creating Demand

Move the Masses to Buy Your Product,
Service, or Idea

The book that shook the marketing world!
Includes:
- The four things people really want.
- Magnetizing your marketing.
- Triggering the purchase decision.
- Double the effectiveness of your advertising at no additional cost.
- Magically attract people to your product or service.
- Preparing your product or service for lift-off.
- Putting people in Decision Making Mode.
- Spread demand throughout the population (or your target market).
- Get them to buy more, more often.

Practical Wisdom

Quotes and Comments That Inspire,
Enlighten, and Entertain

A collection of powerful sayings from many diverse people, living and dead. Wonderful insights about life, love, business, and achievement. Rick Ott has captured the wisdom from each, explaining them in practical, relevant terms.

A fun and interesting read. Randomly flip to any page — the quote you select may very well be the most relevant to you at this time. These people are speaking to you and affecting your life right now!

Paperback; 100 pages
ISBN: 0-9663491-7-7
$10. U.S. $14 CANADA

Creating Demand (Audio program)

Hear Rick Ott explain the most powerful Creating Demand strategies in this 6-CD audio program.

Recorded at the Nightingale-Conant studios in Chicago . . . and what a fun session that was! You'll really enjoy listening, and profiting from the easy-to-understand, easy-to-implement techniques.

Six audio CDs
Includes a bonus workbook on CD-ROM

Available at nightingale.com or 1-800-525-9000

Unleashing Your Productivity (Audio program)

Six audio CDs
Includes a bonus workbook on CD-ROM

This personal development program is not like anything else you've ever heard. In typical Rick Ott contrarian style, Rick explains how to vaporize worry, overcome negative emotions, and cure When Disease. He tells you why visualization doesn't work most of the time, but how to make it work for you. And a whole lot more.

Available at nightingale.com or 1-800-525-9000

Rick Ott

Rick Ott is a professional speaker, author, actor, money manager, graphic designer, and martial artist. He holds a B.A. in Advertising from Michigan State University, an M.B.A. from Virginia Commonwealth University, and a Black Belt from Grandmaster Dong's Martial Arts.

www.rickott.com